Linocuts and Woodcuts

Linocuts
and Woodcuts

a complete block printing handbook

by MICHAEL ROTHENSTEIN

Studio Vista

For ROBERT ERSKINE

© Michael Rothenstein 1962

Pictures by Picasso, Matisse and Vlaminck   © S.P.A.D.E.M., Paris, 1962

Published 1962 in London by Studio Vista Limited

Blue Star House, Highgate Hill, N 19

Reprinted 1965

Set in 11-pt. Plantin, 2-pt. leaded

Made and printed in Great Britain by STAPLES PRINTERS LTD *at their Rochester, Kent, establishment*

Contents

List of Illustrations

FIGURES

Bibliography

About Prints by Stanley William Hayter. Oxford University Press, London, 1962.
   Authoritative background comment on modern printmaking.

Artists' Prints in Colour by Hans Platte. Barrie and Rockcliff, London, 1961.
   Many fine prints are reproduced.

Creative Printmaking by Peter Green. Batsford, London, 1964.
   A brilliant, extensively illustrated work on relief techniques for schools.

Etching and Engraving by John Buckland Wright. Studio Publications, London and New York, 1953.
   A useful and sympathetic study of the techniques of print-making, with a section on wood and linocutting.

The Expressionists by Carl Zigrosser. Thames and Hudson, London, 1957.
   Contains good examples of German Expressionist prints.

The Floating World by James Michener. Random House, New York, and Secker and Warburg, London, 1954.
   An entertaining semi-popular book on Japanese colour prints, full of engaging information on both the prints and the arists.

Graphik des deutschen Expressionismus by Lothar-Guenther Buchheim. Buchheim Verlag, Feldafing, Germany, 1959.
   Contains a magnificent series of reproductions of German Expressionist prints.

Modern Japanese Prints by Oliver Statler. Charles E. Tuttle Company, Vermont, U.S.A., 1956.
   A useful account of some leading Japanese print-makers.

The Modern Woodcut by Herbert Furst. John Lane, London, 1924
   A curious 'period' book with some unexpected reproductions.

New Ways of Gravure by Stanley William Hayter. Routledge and Kegan Paul, London, and Panther Books, New York, 1949.
   Though this includes no direct reference to wood or linocutting, it gives essential information and comment on the practice of print-making in general.

Printing Explained by Herbert Simon and Harry Carter. The Dryad Press, Leicester, England, 1931.
   Contains an excellent description of the working and construction of the Albion press.

Printing Inks by R. Burns. Sir Isaac Pitman, London, 1947.
   A short and clear description of the nature of printing inks.

Printmaking by Gabor Peterdi. The Macmillan Company, New York, 1959.
   Perhaps the most informative and up-to-date book on the various print techniques; contains an excellent section on woodcutting.

Printmaking To-day by Jules Heller. University of California and Sir Isaac Pitman, New York and London, 1958.
   A highly informative account of the techniques and materials used in print-making.

Shiko Munakata by Yoyuro Yasyada. Charles E. Tuttle Company, Vermont, U.S.A., and Tokyo, 1958.
   Short account of the life of Munakata, with reproductions in black-and-white and colour.

Timbers for Woodwork, edited by J. C. S. Brough. Evans Brothers, London, 1947.
   Contains some useful general information about the different timbers.

Tools for Woodwork by Charles H. Hayward. Evans Brothers, London, 1946.
   Practical general account of the tools used in woodworking, of particular use to those specialising in the woodcut.

What Wood is That? by Dr. Alfred Schwankl. Thames and Hudson, London, 1956.
   Contains actual wood samples, in veneer form, together with descriptions of the working properties.

Woodcuts by John R. Biggs. Blandford Press, London, 1958.
   A technically valuable book with a good section on using the Albion press.

Acknowledgements

I want to thank the following artists for permission to reproduce their work: Edward Bawden; Antonio Frasconi; Gertrude Hermes; Seong Moy; Adja Yunkers. Acknowledgements are also due to the Museum of Modern Art, New York; the Stedelijk Museum, Amsterdam; and the Victoria and Albert Museum, London, for permission to reproduce prints from their collections; to the Hanover Gallery, St. George's Gallery, and Zwemmer Gallery, London, and the Galerie Louise Leiris, Paris, for lending either photographs or prints; and to the Buchheim Verlag, Munich, for permission to reproduce prints.

Grateful thanks are also due to Michael Johnson for particular trouble taken over photographs of both studio and equipment; to Mrs. Molly Hamling for the careful typing and revision of the text; to Miss Anne Petrides for lending many books on print-making and related subjects from Camberwell Art School Library; to my colleagues at Camberwell Art School, Theo Mendes, Geoffrey Hoare, Peter Weaver and Frank Martin for giving information about the teaching methods they use, and for lending their students' work; to Roger Sullock and Ronald King for collecting and loaning work from their own classes at Camberwell Art School; to Miss Sheila Robinson for lending work by her students at Walthamstow Technical College; to the Hon. Robert Erskine and Anne Leane for help in tracing some of the prints and other materials needed. I should also like to mention R. Burns' book *Printing Inks*, an excellent short account which was a great help to me in writing of this subject, and to acknowledge help from Ronald Horton's article *Experiments with Materials* which appeared in *Education and Art*, a Unesco publication, in writing the *Techniques for Schools* section. My thanks are also due to my wife for many useful suggestions.

Photographs of tools and equipment by Michael Johnson
Line drawings by Frank Johnson

Approach to Print-making

This book is addressed to the professional artist, the student, and the teacher. In any case the interests of both professional and teacher are, in the main, identified, since the free-lance artist may also teach, and equally the teacher make prints. The amateur print-maker, too, must be considered, though his needs may stand in a rather separate and simpler category; but I hope to serve his interests as well.

In writing something about wood and lino cutting at the present time one has the hope of reaching both a larger and more intelligent audience than would have existed even a few years ago. In schools, in dealers' galleries, above all in the large international exhibitions, the interest in the colour print has shown steady growth: an interest not restricted to any one country or group of countries. This vitality has brought a new sophistication of means; the old sharply defined frontiers have been broken down. To-day many artists take naturally to combined processes; images from metal, wood and lino combined in a single print.

The professional artist, earning his living by the editions that he prints, is likely to have a large workshop and a great deal of equipment, but good prints can also be made with the simplest tools and materials; a piece of ordinary lino or unwanted plank, a sharp knife, an ink roller – or home-made dabber – and a tube of printing ink. Again, the professional is likely to operate a printing press, but the student or amateur can print effectively with the back of a tablespoon.

We may well ask, however, why an artist should want to produce prints, to engrave on wood or linoleum rather than to use oil paint on canvas. It is true that prints are often made for reasons of professional expediency, to serve a sector of the artist's public that cannot buy his work in the normal way. A print at five guineas can be acquired by a hundred where only one could afford an original work of sculpture or painting. Though this is a plausible enough reason for a well-known artist to produce a print, it clearly fails to touch the question 'why we do prints' on any fundamental level.

Among a wealth of reasons – the active character of printed shapes, boldness of design, clarity of colour – we shall, I believe, get closest to an answer if we consider the engraved line and carved shape as the basic characteristics of the print. Here in a special sense is the nerve of the question touched, for the carving of a line or shape demands quite different gestures to those we make with a brush or pen. The knife must always be drawn through the wood towards the body, an action that may indeed call on all one's strength; while the gouge or graver must always be pushed away. In contrast the hand that grasps a brush or pencil can move quickly and freely in any direction; the gestures are unrestricted and may, if necessary, be executed with speed. Channelling lines from the face of a tough resistant material, on the other hand, is slow and sometimes laborious. The nervous and muscular effort entailed gives the line a certain rigidity, often a square-cut chunkiness in complete contrast to the free trace of a crayon, brush or pen. But the mark these drawing instruments leave behind is without physical depth; it is a two-dimensional track, inscribed without muscular effort, on the surface of canvas or paper. The line cut in depth possesses an element of authority; and its very nature, powerful, simple and severe, may hope to celebrate a certain mastery over a tough material. It also suggests the character of permanence; a connection with the incised legend on the hard material of wall or monument. This incised line is something that engraving shares with some of the earliest expressions of form that have come down to us from primitive man. The engraved lines left on the rock face invariably interact in some way with the relief, the shifts of plane, of the rock itself. Perhaps the contour expressive of a bull's shoulder and back follows, at some point, a slight projecting shelf of limestone; or the bulk of a horse's body may be expressed partly by a swelling face of rock and partly by the engraved line by which it is enclosed.

The desire to cut signs or images into the mass of a tough material would appear to answer some instinctive need. A boy will always find pleasure in carving his name on the flap of the desk, and perhaps the difficulty of cutting this with his knife, once crowned with success, will lead to further rudimentary embellishments. In the poorer quarters of many towns one notices too how someone who waits habitually on a particular street corner will be tempted to incise his initials, a heart, or the name of a girl, on the plaster of an adjacent wall.

I would like to call attention to a further characteristic of print-making: one that in itself might attract many artists at the present time. I refer to the special experience of conspiring with some organic material, such as wood, to produce a work of art. It is clear that this applies peculiarly to the woodcut, and only then when the figure, texture or grain structure of the timber becomes fully integrated with the scheme of the design. When this occurs the material of the block itself becomes, in a very real sense, a part of the subject. And here a further starting point is provided for an art where the hand need not always intervene.

In all printing the film of ink impressed upon the paper is extremely thin when compared to the pigment flowing from a loaded brush. The tension, rhythm and direction of the slight ridges and furrows left by the brush mark will always reinforce the vitality and intention of the gesture that produced it. Transferred to paper by pressure alone the ink carries no direct impress of the artist's hand. A print, more perhaps than any other medium, depends peculiarly on the overall power of its design. Unless its structure possesses exceptional authority and firmness – to compensate for this evident lack of surface variety – the print is likely to be without life or character.

It is always dangerous for the artist to base a print too closely on a drawn or painted original. In painting, as we have seen, the stroke comes from the brush, often lightly held; but in carving forceful gestures and a rigid tool are used. The character of the stroke should come from the knife or gouge, from the feel of the blade as it moves through the resistant material.

Too much calculation will kill the pleasure in carving your block, but if your attack is bold and free the discipline of the material will impose itself naturally. The print-maker has no call to be aware of undue restraint. Work done with decision will get back a clear echo from the limitations of the medium.

The colour of a print always retains a certain formality, since the different colours are put down separately and do not mix. This has sometimes led us to regard the print-maker's film of pigment as a poor man's substitute – stiff, restrained and thin – for the opulence of oil paint. But thinness of ink does not proclude richness of colour. The colour of a good print is something on its own and works its own way. Decision and formality reveal unexpected qualities; in the linocuts of Picasso it may be the strict unyielding gravity of black and the earth colours; in Joan Miro's metal relief prints the heraldic brilliance of blue, orange and red; in the woodcuts of Kirchner and Nolde the flaring contrasts of sunset.

Although in Paris woodcuts and linocuts are occasionally printed by the professional printer, here in England, and in most countries abroad, the various stages of the edition, from block to print, are carried through by the artist in his own studio. But contrary to what one might expect this condition carries many advantages. Printing on his own brings the artist close to the job; much closer than if professional help were used. Indeed, it would be true to say that without this extension into the printed image the act of cutting the block is finally seen as something incomplete. In the woodcuts and linocuts of Munakata, Gauguin or Kirchner, the relief of the block is completely understood in relation to the printed image. There is a true organic connection between the cutting of the block and the way the carved forms receive the ink from the roller; a complete unity of means that only the few, outstanding print-makers achieve.

In Great Britain, in contrast to Germany, America and France, the recent history of linocutting and woodcutting suggests that too much fuss and attention may well have been paid to these mediums considered as highly specialized crafts that draw their interest largely from purely professional know-how and skill. But I do not feel they should be seen in this light. On the contrary, once we accept them as legitimate means of original expression, their results should be judged, as they are judged in painting and sculpture, by virtue of this quality above all else. Some of the most powerful prints, such as the linocuts of Matisse and Picasso, have been cut directly upon the block, as directly as we would approach a sheet of paper and make a pen drawing. The gesture throughout is wonderfully direct and free, although the lines are gouged and grooved from a tough, intractable material. Although more limited in scope, prints taken from lino and wood are not fundamentally different from painting and drawing at the aesthetic level. Even though dealing with difficult materials, and sometimes laborious techniques, the print-maker should attack his block, whenever possible, with something of the unrestrained excitement we associate more commonly with the painter's mood and temper.

Prints travel easily. Single copies can be put into cardboard tubes, and whole editions are easily packed between boards. Nor need their distribution wait on formal occasions for exhibition. As they are produced by the artist they may be sent to the dealer, where we can go to see them, often within a few weeks of their first production. In this way prints make a special contribution to the art of our own time; through woodcuts, engravings and lithographs we are able to keep in touch, from year to year, with the work of many of the finest living artists – Tamayo in Mexico, Dubuffet in France, Munakata in Tokyo – quite independently of the publication of books or the mounting of exhibitions.

I made the comment earlier that I believed the English tend to reverence craft too much for its own sake, and this criticism might also be made with regard to certain tendencies in the teaching of print-making. It may well be that the special prestige which still attaches to the severe discipline of engraving – engraving on end-grain boxwood in the strict sense – has tended to exert a rather inhibiting influence on the activities of the print class. Too often one has seen only small black-and-white prints coming from the art room; often of fairgrounds, circuses and children playing in park or street – prints that may bear no relation to the direction in which print methods are moving in the mainstream of development. A moment's reflection on the range of recent graphic art will attest the part played by new materials, and new technical approaches. One feels inevitably that the student, even the young student, should in no way be excluded from the vigour and exhilaration of the prevailing atmosphere.

14

1 · Workshop

One must be wary in discussing studio or workshop arrangements; planning will depend to a great extent on the quirks of personal convenience. Advice too easily has the ring of an intrusion, unwanted in a private world, whether one considers the comparatively complex set-up of the professional print-maker or the simpler situation of the amateur or student. It cannot be overstressed, however, that good work can be produced with the simplest means.

Broadly speaking, one can say that everything related to printing should be arranged round the printing table or the press; and everything related to designing and cutting the blocks round the worktable. Work in colour involves several different processes that are closely interlinked; ideally each needs its own work area and storage for the appropriate tools, materials and equipment.

The worktable should be large, with solid legs, and should stand, if possible, in direct left-hand sidelight. It should be high enough to work at either standing, without stooping, or while sitting on a high stool. If your table is too low you should have the legs extended or jack them up with bricks or woodblocks.

The level of your eyes should be at sufficient height above the table to enable you to look down on the block, so that you can assess shapes without the distortion due to foreshortening. Your block, for the same reason, should rest on a drawing board, sloped at a convenient angle on a block of wood.

Storage of all tools and materials needed for the design and preparation of the blocks should be kept within easy reach of this table. A power point for the electric sander – the purpose of this valuable tool is later described – should also be adjacent.

Another requirement of the studio, and this will apply equally to the art class, is a flat wide sink with both hot and cold water. This will be in constant use for the various cleaning jobs that printing entails.

Although to begin with you can proof effectively without a press, by burnishing the back of your print with a spoon, or by standing or stamping on the back of the block in the case of lino, a method described in the 'printing' section, a press is necessary for printed work on any serious scale. This should be an Albion or press of similar platen type. The hand rubbing of large blocks is too laborious to be really practical, especially for printing editions in colour. The Columbian press is still occasionally used in England as well as the Albion, but the Albion is more common; while in America the Washington press is the one most often found. It is doubtful if any of these presses are being made today. If you buy one through a dealer, even though it is reconditioned – secondhand, it may still be very expensive. You will do better to advertise in a printers' 'Sales and Wants' paper, or an art journal such as the *Arts Review*. But one of the best ways of acquiring a press is to attend a printing-works auction. The commercial printer often regards the Albion as a piece of obsolete equipment, taking up space that could be better used. In consequence a fine press may fetch a few pounds only.

The smaller Albions have short legs and are made to stand on a bench; the larger ones are the right height for use when standing on the ground. An effective Albion press for printing wood and linocuts of any size is a heavy piece of equipment – a press with a platen 11″ × 16″ weighs at least 4 cwt., and a large press much more. A Super-royal, size 27″ × 21″, may weigh over half a ton. The frame, known as the staple, always cast in a single piece, is heavy to lift and difficult to handle. Should a press be acquired at an auction sale it may well need professional help for removal, transport and setting up. My own press, for example, a magnificent Albion, dating from 1888, with a bed 28″ × 40″, cost five pounds at a London sale, but the transit and installation was over forty.

If the large Albion is to stand on any but a ground or basement floor it will need to stand on 'spreaders'; pieces of timber 2″ × 4″ that will spread the weight of the press across the floor joists. The timber must therefore run at right angles to the direction of the joists.

To operate the Albion your block is placed on the bed of the press and run under the platen by turning a handle. The hand lever is now pulled; this forces a wedge inside the press into an upright position and the platen descends on your block with great force.

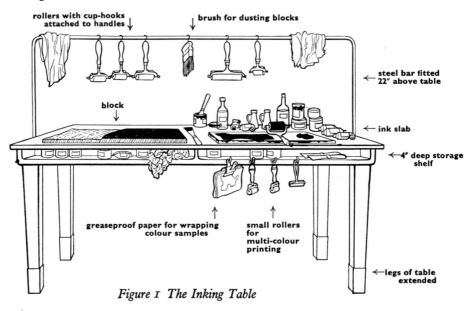

Figure 1 The Inking Table

The tympan is a metal frame, hinged to the bed, covered with a tight skin of either vellum or linen. For wood and lino printing its purpose is to control the thickness of packing used above the block. The more sophisticated functions of the tympan, when used with a frisket, are not required for the printing methods described here. For more detailed information about the construction and working of the platen press refer to *Printing Explained* by Herbert Simon and Harry Carter, Dryad Press 1931, or *Woodcuts* by John R. Biggs, Blandford Press 1958; or consult an experienced printer.

It should be strongly stressed that the big press has many advantages over the small one. You should get the largest that your pocket and studio space allow. For work of any size the press can hardly be too big. The larger the press the less the effort that is needed to print, for your strength is many times multiplied by the leverage of its movement.

In the art school the presses are very rarely of sufficient power. The teacher should remember that if breakdowns are to be avoided the press must be strong enough to withstand the inexpert and sometimes ruthless methods of the average student.

A stout wooden block should be fixed firmly to the floor beneath the track of the press. This is placed so that the right foot, pressed against it, gains sufficient leverage to enable you to pull the arm of the press without strain. For a large press the proper movement is to push against the floorblock, throwing the weight of your body sharply backwards with the arms extended, the lever gripped with both hands as near the end as convenient, much as you would grip a single oar in rowing.

Though much less practical, it is also possible to take prints from plywood and linoleum blocks from an etching press – but not plankwood as this is normally too thick. When lino is used strips of wood should be glued to a sheet of backing paper which is put on the bed of the press. The strips should be the height of the block and run on either side of the block parallel with the length of the bed. If you fail to do this the lino, being elastic, may stretch, going out of register, under pressure of the roller. In any case the screws in the frame of the press, which control the pressure of the upper roller, should be unscrewed until the roller itself runs free over your block entirely on its own weight.

The inking table, like the worktable, should be high enough to work at without stooping; it should stand as near the press as convenience will allow – not more than three or four steps distant if waste effort is to be avoided. The inking slab should consist either of a thick piece of plate glass or a piece of white or light coloured marble. Old marble table tops make excellent ink slabs, and they can still be bought from junk dealers for a few shillings. If glass is used, a sheet of white paper is put underneath. The average roller is either 4″ or 6″ wide; for colour printing the slab should be wide enough to roll out at least three colours at any one time.

When you are printing a great deal of time is spent in cleaning – blocks, rollers and the ink slab need wiping down each time new colours are used. Cleaning fluids in containers with sprinkler tops such as bottles with punctured metal caps, easily grasped in the hand, should be kept within easy reach. These are filled and replenished from larger containers, such as gallon cans, conveniently stored under the worktable. Low grade commercial petrol is probably the best cleaning fluid for the studio but being highly inflammable it should never be used in the art class. White spirit or blue or pink paraffin is used when you need a cleaner that does not evaporate quickly.

Though the student or amateur can spread his sheets to dry on the table, the best equipment for holding the prints when they are drying is a ball-clip rack that may be suspended from the ceiling or hung along the wall. These frames are sold in six foot lengths and are obtainable from Hunter-Penrose in London and from most large printing equipment dealers elsewhere.

Prints may also be stacked on nests of hardboard trays, but these are rather cumbersome to move and take up a good deal of space.

For many jobs in the print studio metal weights are used in preference to drawing pins; they keep tracings in position on the block and hold the print in register when you are burnishing. Weights are quickly handled and leave no pin marks. Your local garage – or blacksmith if you live in remote country – should give you all the metal scrap you need.

A good way to keep tools within easy reach is to put them on the shelves of an ordinary two-tier food trolley. This can be moved conveniently as you work and pushed out of the way when you need clear space. Line the trays with bits of blanket or felt, as all tools with a cutting edge should be kept on a soft or padded surface.

The whole arrangement of the studio should be planned to save your labour. When you use large blocks, in particular, you may find the calls on your strength considerable; strain will follow unless the studio floorspace has been intelligently planned. At the outset of a day's printing all your gear – paper, inks, rollers, rags, cleaning fluids – should be placed in position, and the track of the press should be generously oiled. Even a small edition of twenty-five prints, in four colours, will mean that the printing cycle – inking of blocks, registration and handling of the sheets – will be repeated at least one hundred times. To do this successfully a continuous unhurried rhythm must be built up and steadily maintained.

18

2 · Tools

Gouges and knives are the basic tools for both wood and lino cutting. In size the gouges vary from small V tools – scrivers – used for hairlike lines to large wood carving tools, mounted in short handles, used for clearing background material. Those fitted like a pen-nib in a handle are to be avoided. Unfortunately, on account of low cost, they are used frequently in schools; but the thin blade, a tin-like meagre instrument, quickly works loose in the handle. The moment this happens all sense of touch is destroyed and loose and careless cutting will result. It is better to buy three or four good gouges than a dozen cheaper ones.

The gouge is held with the handle-end comfortably cupped in your palm. As the tool enters the wood the stroke will move away from your body. If you are right-handed a long cut will also tend to move diagonally towards the left; but as the block is freely turned at any angle to the tool there is no real restriction on the direction of your cut.

Your knife may be a Stanley knife, mounted with a heavy-duty blade, or one of Japanese or English pattern. It may even be an ordinary pocket-knife bound with string for convenient gripping.

The English, Stanley or pocket-knife is either held with an overhand grip, rather as you would hold the end of a stick to deliver a blow, or as a pen is held. The Japanese is grasped as you would hold a dagger, with your thumb over the handle-end.

The V tool cuts a channel at a single stroke, the knife cuts one side only. The knife is usually held in the hand to make a diagonal cut of some 45 degrees; turning the block the other way round, a second cut at the same angle, removes a V shaped sliver of wood.

The point of the knife can also be used for scratching or scoring lines on the face of the block, before the later stage of deep cutting begins – much as you would use pencil or charcoal before starting to paint.

For cutting a close system of fine lines the multiple tool is employed. This tool cuts well on linoleum but is less effective on side-grain wood. But in addition to those already mentioned many sorts of tool can be used. It will be obvious that anything capable of cutting, scratching, bruising and denting the wood – a hammer blow, the point of a nail, even the stroke of a hard pencil – will produce a printed image. There are few limits to the methods that can be used – but it is clear that only the final quality of the work will justify their use.

Gouges and knives are sharpened on ordinary artificial stones, axolite, carborundum or India, and are finished with Arkansas or Washita for greater keenness. For woodcutting the tool must be razor sharp and should be stropped in addition. Any piece of soft leather will make a strop; it should be rubbed over with razor strop paste obtainable from most good tool or cutlery stores.

The tool is sharpened or stropped during work the moment the edge is dull. This should be done frequently; a blunt tool is quite unresponsive and will kill the nerve of your touch. Test for sharpness either by feeling the edge carefully across your finger tip, or by looking down at the edge when the tool is held pointing to the light. It is dull if any light is reflected.

The sharpening of all hollow tools needs practice. The main difficulty is keeping the tool at a steady angle. This is partly overcome if you make a habit of putting the stone in the same place in relation to your body each time it is used; wrist and arm then tend to take up the habitual position relative to the stone. The method is either to roll the tool between your fingers, or to rotate the wrist as the edge passes across the stone, so that the whole curve is sharpened evenly. You may use either a push-and-pull movement or a slightly rotary one.

A slip-stone is used to sharpen the inside of the hollow gouge, but as it is pressed level with the metal the function is mainly to remove the burr raised by honing the outside curve. It is passed either along the edge from side to side, or up and down, holding the stone flat against the inside curve. The slip is a wedge-shaped stone, generally made of axolite, sharp on one side for the V tool and rounded on the other for the gouge.

The V tool must be sharpened on both sides, holding the bevel flat against the stone; but the meeting point of the two sides is ground as for a fine hollow gouge. This is the critical point and must be done with great care. Any failure to do this will result in the cut tearing the wood, used crossgrain, or jumping and slipping when used on linoleum.

20

For the largest gouges and for wood-carving tools the basic method is reversed and the stone is rubbed against the tool. The stone is grasped and rubbed against the bevel of the tool, which is held stationary in the other hand. The length of the bevel should be carefully maintained.

Plenty of oil is put on the stone. Particles of steel, which come off during sharpening, float in the oil and can afterwards be wiped away. With too little oil these particles stay on the stone, which soon becomes glazed. Thin machine oil or salad oil is used; added paraffin helps to keep the natural stones from clogging. These should be cleaned after use.

When the gouge has been repeatedly sharpened the edge may be worn and irregular; it is then necessary to re-grind the tool. The gouge is held at a right angle to the flat of the grindstone if the edge only is to be ground, and at the necessary angle if the bevel is to be followed. If the edge is only slightly worn it can be ground on a fast cutting oil stone, such as carborundum, by holding the tool upright and rotating firmly until the wandering edge of the tool is ground straight.

Ordinary carpentry tools are used to some extent in woodcutting. Wood needs sawing to size and planing back or front if the plank is warped. The electric sander is another tool of the utmost value: for certain jobs it is indispensable. On plywood it will reduce the roughness of background wood, cleared with the gouge, quickly and easily and can be used on the printing surface itself to give small variations in height of plane, too fine to be practical for the gouge. Such variations enable you to reduce or graduate the tone over chosen areas of your print. The circular-saw attachment is excellent for cutting both ply and plankwood rapidly. The cut being a true right-angle to the face of the wood is also a great advantage where blocks are made up from more than one piece.

Cramps will be needed to lock the wood in position while cutting, or they may be used to fix a piece of wood at the top of your board to act as a bench stop. This prevents the block from slipping as you work. For small cuts the wood is kept still by the pressure of the left hand, but care should be taken to keep the hand clear of the direction in which your stroke is running. Whenever possible the hand is kept *behind* the edge of the tool; in a class for young students it is essential to explain this relationship of the two hands, the block-holding hand and the tool-holding hand, with the firmest emphasis.

3 · Materials

At the present time an enormous range of materials for block-making is open to the print-maker. Some are expensive, such as prepared fruitwood blocks bought from a dealer, others are easily found or cost very little – a plywood picture back or unwanted plank – and these are specially useful to the student or amateur. No material of any practical value should be despised; only your talent will define the limits of achievement whatever materials you use.

Very broadly speaking we can divide these materials into two groups: those with a smooth surface or little perceptible texture, and those with strong surface character and marked texture. Materials with a smooth finish include linoleum, hardboard and planed wood with close even grain. For detailed work a smooth surface and a fairly hard material is necessary. In this case blocks of planed fruitwood are chosen, certain kinds of veneered wood or thick hard linoleum that has been scraped smooth with the flat of a knife. Materials with a strong texture, however, are suitable for broadly cut work, for blocks on a large scale or for prints where texture or vigorous surface treatment plays a fundamental part in your design. Such materials include unplaned or machine planed wood and planks of strong natural grain; in special cases they may even include wood that has been exposed to the effects of weathering or contains the whorls of large knots or shakes – the splits and fissures due to shrinkage.

Linoleum

Linoleum is a much more remarkable medium than many suppose. Its humble association with the school art class, and the flat and arty vision that work in this medium may suggest, have both tended to give an entirely false view of its capabilities. Many fine artists, Picasso and Matisse among them, have shown how much expression linoleum engraving can possess: Picasso in particular with his large series of lino colour-prints executed in the years 1959–60. These images were mostly taken from a single block, a method of printing, stage by stage, as areas of the linoleum are successively cut away.

Linoleum is easy to cut and may be cut in any direction; it is splendidly adapted to direct clear drawing and hard edges. It is a superb medium for the use of colour.

Further, linoleum is a living material, more so than many imagine. When new it may be dull enough, it has a disagreeable softness; but with use it hardens, absorbing oil from the inks. The surface is further improved by the friction of repeated cleaning. Finally it may take on a rich polish, like the surface of old leather or even bronze. To handle and print such material can give as much pleasure as if the block were a well-grained piece of wood.

A vigorously cut piece of linoleum stands punishing wear. I have had machine editions of over three thousand copies taken from a single set of blocks.

If not thickly inked lino will print with a perceptible grain, a fine speckled texture that is sometimes of considerable interest.

An ideal thickness for linoleum is $\frac{3}{8}''$. This is not as expensive as Battleship – the thickest – but is still thick enough for the most vigorous cutting, using large gouges or woodcutting tools. Thin lino has a meagre feel under the tool; it is more difficult to cut back freely, the gouge reaching the canvas too soon. It is, however, useful for flat simple areas of colour.

To get lino cheaply you should buy offcuts or trimmings from a big store; these are odd widths, leftovers from flooring cut to order, and are much less expensive than linoleum bought by the yard.

The lino should be plain in colour – any plain colour – and not inlaid. If you buy a quantity it will be rolled in transit; it should be unpacked on arrival and laid flat on the studio floor. If this is not done quickly the curvature is difficult to straighten later, and the lino must be perfectly flat for convenient work.

New lino is often too soft, but if it is laid on the floor, stood upon and walked over, the surface will toughen and harden. Minute scratches do not matter if your work is broad in treatment and large in scale. If, on the other hand, you wish for perfect smoothness you should scrape the surface with the flat of a razor blade before starting work.

Old lino, on the other hand, may get too hard, especially in cold weather. Should this occur you can put it to warm near a stove or out in the sun.

Hardboard

Hardboard is another practical material especially for students; it is less expensive than either linoleum or wood. It is too thin, however, to be cut in depth and has neither the texture of lino nor the variety of wood. Hardboard is perhaps most useful to the professional for a single printing, used in combination with other materials. In the hands of Edward Middleditch, however, hardboard has proved a most impressive material (Plate 19).

Plankwood

Of all the materials discussed here plankwood, wood cut in the direction of the grain, has the strongest character. It is the classic medium for the print taken from a carved block.

Broadly speaking wood is divided into two classes, hardwoods and softwoods. The hardwoods come from the trees that have broad flat leaves, such as oak, apple or chestnut, which shed their foliage in the autumn. The softwoods come from trees with narrow resinous leaves and include the various types of pine. The latter have a simpler cell structure and date their origins from a more remote period in the history of our planet. The terms hardwood and softwood are to some extent misleading; the hardest softwood is harder than the softest hardwood.

Of the hardwoods alone over two thousand varieties have been listed, though comparatively few have been in common use for print-making – the enterprising print-maker, however, may well be tempted to experiment with new varieties in the future.

Selection of wood will depend first on its fitness for the particular block required. But your decision will also be influenced by the cost, availability, and by its working properties.

Grain will normally apply to markings on the end of the wood, cross sawn. Figure applies to the length grain and is affected by the mode of cutting from the log, such terms as curly, wavy, spiral, straight and interlocked are used to describe its character.

If your block needs close, precise or detailed cutting the timber should be free of knots and possess an even grain. Among softwoods white and yellow pine and Parana pine, which has an exceptionally even texture, are all excellent. Among hardwoods, sycamore, lime and maple are used; but the fruitwoods, such as pear and cherry, that cut sharp and sweet in each direction, have been chiefly favoured in the past. Siebolds beech, Katsura, Lanan, silver magnolia, and basswood are among those chosen by the Japanese.

Bought from the artist's dealer, however, planed fruitwood blocks are apt to be small and expensive. Unless a perfectly smooth surface is needed, timber should be obtained straight from the woodyard. Most artists and students today seek the greater freedom of larger blocks and of fairly low priced timber.

24

PLATE I Printing Table. The ink slab is on the right. Working surface is kept clear but rollers, cleaning fluids and rags are kept within easy reach.

PLATE 2 The Albion Press.

PLATE 3　Gouges, oil stones and slip-stone; a multiple tool, Japanese knife and Stanley knife are shown in the bottom row.

PLATE 4　Two weathered boards attached to a back-board. Any fragments of wood or lino used like this can be accurately registered.

PLATE 5 Set of blocks with finished proof. Top, weathered boards and plywood block for all-over tone. Bottom, carved plankwood block and proof.

Figure 2 Image taken from weathered elm

Most timber research and development centres, such as the Forest Products Research Laboratory, Princes Risborough in England will give information relating to all the main types of timber.

One of the unique qualities of the print consists of the power to combine blocks of a different order into a single image; a highly worked block closely gouged and engraved, with another chosen for surface vitality alone; or a block of rough, open, horizontal grain, with one whose texture is close, silky and vertical in movement.

If you want blocks with strong texture, old and even partly rotten timber can be used. Found on old building sites, or backyards, each plank reveals the ravages of individual history (Figs. 2 and 3). With exposure the grain may be heightened, giving a clear printed image. You may even find that old nail holes or cracked and shrivelled paint yield qualities of unexpected value.

All timber contains moisture, normally from 10 to 25%, much more when the wood is damp. If the old wood you have is damp, it should be stood edgeways near a stove to dry. If you put it facing the source of warmth, the warm side loses

Figure 3 Image taken from pinewood doorpanel

moisture quicker than the cold side and the wood will curl. When this happens, turn it round; the plank should then straighten. Before work the timber must be vigorously cleaned, and dirt or patches of rotten wood brushed away with a stiff wire brush. If you brush in the direction of the grain, the relief is heightened. The surface may also be scrubbed with a pad of steel wool, scouring powder and hot water. If your plank is warped it should be thoroughly wetted: it is then dried out under heavy pressure on a flat surface.

The printing surface of most plankwood is improved if it is sandpapered, and linseed oil rubbed into the grain. In time the oil will harden the wood fibres, making them silky; it also helps the ink to take readily and smoothly in the early stages of proofing.

Plywood

Plywood is an extremely interesting material to the print-maker, largely for the great variety of types that are now available. The cheapest, sometimes known as tea-chest plywood, is too thin to be really practical. Plys with a thick centre layer, known as stoutheart, and the thicker grades of a quarter of an inch and over, known as multi-ply, are all excellent material for blocks.

Plywood is cut with mechanical accuracy and will print admirably in an Albion press. If the ply is thin it may warp with cutting, but to some extent this will straighten under the pressure of the press platen.

In manufacture the wood is 'unwrapped' in a continuous sheet from a tree trunk rotated against a knife, fed forward automatically. The natural figure of the wood is therefore broken up. Each sheet of wood is glued at right angles to the adjacent layers. In using the gouge the different directions of the grain need careful study. In certain kinds of ply this unwrapping process opens the fibre of the wood, producing a finely textured printed image of considerable interest. By contrast pine or birch can be sandpapered to a smooth and silky finish.

Many modern Japanese print-makers use plywood veneered with Katsura, silver magnolia, basswood and other woods that were used in plankwood form by the traditional print-makers.

4 · Work Method

A large steel square is a necessary instrument for cutting either wood or linoleum blocks to size. The method is to true one edge, cut the sides accurately at right angles, and see that the remaining edge is trimmed parallel to the first. To cut linoleum, drive a sharp knife (a Stanley with heavy duty blade is best) two or three times along your straight edge or the edge of your steel square. Now fold the lino back – away from the cut: the remaining thickness will break along the edge. Finally the canvas backing is cut through from the back. When you use colour and need more than one block the lino needs accurate trimming to register the different blocks correctly. The register enables you to position one colour in relation to another when several printings are needed. This is done from one corner and the bottom edge, by pushing the lino flush against stubs of hardboard glued in position on a sheet of stiff paper as shown (Plate 45 and Fig. 5). If you are right-handed use the left-hand bottom corner of the lino, and cut both this corner and the bottom edge as clean as possible; right through the lino with a vertical cut if your hands are strong.

If the colour of your wood or linoleum is light enough to show up your line you are free to draw directly on the face of the block. But when the material is already dark, darken it further with Indian ink used in a swab of cotton wool; a light coloured chalk line or trace will then show clearly.

Follow the same method in transferring your design from a drawing to a dark urface. The line, traced from the original, is repeated on the block with ordinary yellow carbon paper or red chalk lithographic carbon.

When your print is to read the same way round as your drawing, the tracing paper is turned face down on the block, and traced from the back, but if you want your design reversed it is traced from the front. To register your tracing accurately on the block, trim two corners exactly to the block size.

A Biro pen is a good stylo, giving a sharp line through both tracing paper and carbon.

When you want to paint directly on the tracing, making changes or using colour, use diluted printing ink or Magic Marker ink. Water colour or Indian ink cockles the paper, sending it out of register.

Once the drawing or tracing has been established on the wood or lino you are free to commence work on the face of the block. As far as possible make sure of your lines and shapes before carving to any depth, establishing them at first with light lines and marks that do not need deep slivers of material removed. Large areas of material are rarely removed until a working proof has been obtained, especially when cutting blocks for colour. A line can be filled and recut; but it is impractical to fill large cavities left by the gouge.

Strokes on the face of the block can always be scored with the point of a sharp knife – the Japanese knife is excellent for this. Provided your shapes are well defined you are now able to take a proof. This is done by inking normally: wiping back unwanted ink to the scored line.

Another method is to paint directly on the block when only a minimum of cutting has been done. Use a stiff brush and printing ink thinned with a little turpentine. The block is run through the press and a broad image of your print is obtained as a working proof. The ink remaining on the block is either cleaned off or fixed with french chalk or talcum powder. Work can now proceed by further cutting, but this time you are able to take direct account of the pull.

Finally you can try cutting the main block to the stage where it may be inked with a roller in the normal manner. You can now develop the proof using brushes, inks, colour – any materials you wish. Working on the pull directly in this way, you can evolve your idea while keeping it closely in step with work already on the block. The shapes to be retained in your final image are traced off and transferred to a second, third or fourth block, according to the number of colours you need for the completed print.

By inking with small size rollers and brushes several colours can be printed together, but this is only practical if the various colour areas are separate islands on the face of the block. When the forms are close to each other, bunched together on the surface of the block, you can only proof by inking and printing two or three colours at a time. For further colours the block is again run through the press, the printing proceeding in separate stages.

To avoid unnecessary tracing, the image on your first block may be reproduced on the others by offsetting. To do this a heavily-inked black proof is laid face downward, in register, on the second block and pulled through the press. The dark image should show up clearly on the lighter colour of your wood or lino. The ink may be immediately dried with chalk or powder and the cutting of your new block begun.

The Cutting

Any material removed from the wood or lino leaves a white, unprinted, line or shape upon the proof. This is the basic principle of the relief block; the roller in passing over the surface cannot now reach its lower level, the top surface alone receiving ink.

While the V tool cuts a channel at a single stroke, the knife as we have seen cuts one side only. The knife angle is lowered to widen the cut. Some print-makers, keeping the block the same way round, reverse the angle of the knife, using a backhand stroke for the second cut. To cut effectively, sink the point of the knife in the wood and draw it towards you using the pressure of your whole body and not the arm alone.

Large areas of wood or lino are quickly cleared with large curved gouges; ridges left can be levelled with the flatter ones. But systematic clearing may be detrimental, as printed indications of the background cutting may add interest and tension to your print.

It may be useful to remember, however, that the roller, in passing over the wood, needs adequate support to run clear of the lowered surfaces. Where such support is not given, the carving of the background should be strong and deep.

A downward slanting grain may cause the tool to enter the wood too steeply. When this happens it is advisable to start cutting from the opposite direction. Normally, however, no consistent attempt is made to cut with the grain, but you are likely to find greater control and smoother carving if grain direction is followed.

Unwanted lines or holes on the block can be filled with a mixture of plaster of Paris and glue, plastic wood or any stopper that dries hard and firm. For the most part these materials tend to shrink during the drying process, so the cavity should be filled 'proud' – slightly higher than the existing surface of the block – and sandpapered level when dry.

To achieve gradation of tone, sandpaper is often used on the woodblock; but the electric sander is a far more effective instrument. The method is to keep the block in position with cramp or weights. The sander, firmly gripped in both hands, is gently swept from side to side across the plane to be lowered. A fine disk should be used: sawdust can be cleaned from the disk with india rubber.

Though wood can be delicately modulated by sanding and shaving with the extra flat gouge the surface of lino is more intractable. Variations are obtained by pitting and cutting with fine gouges or with the multiple tool which should be held firmly and used with a clean strong stroke.

Texture

If you have an etching press you can pit large areas of lino by sweeping coarse sand, rather sparingly where required, and running the block through the press under heavy pressure. A sheet of thin metal, such as an old lithoplate, should be put above the block to keep the grains in place and the press roller undamaged and clean. When printed this achieves the effect of a rough aquatint surface.

Built-up solid texture, using a plastic substance such as plaster and glue, provides one of the most interesting developments of the lino block. This material can be brushed and spread on the block; freely drawn into with a point or treated by any method you would use to work or texture a soft plastic surface. It will also take the impress of any suitable object pressed into it while malleable: but once set and dry it becomes bone hard and can be carved, sandpapered or filed. If drastic alteration is needed it should be thoroughly wetted and removed by scraping.

The method is to heat strong glue in any form of double boiler, but an iron glue pot that will keep it warm while you work is far the most convenient. Pearl glue soaked in a little water for an hour is ready for heating. It is then poured warm into a second vessel containing the plaster; and here again an iron gluepot is a great advantage. The dental plaster of Paris, bought at any chain store chemist is excellent quality.

Before applying the gesso, the lino surface must be perfectly clean; scrub it with sandpaper or steel wool, using hot water and scouring powder. The block is first brushed over with glue, and the mixture, which must be kept warm during use, is stirred quickly and evenly together before use. It should have the consistency of thick paste and is freely spread with a palette knife or large stiff brush.

The glue-plaster should take about twelve hours to dry. If the texture has a pronounced tooth it will need smoothing with sandpaper before rolling up with ink. Glue-gesso stands up well to the pressure of the press and large editions may be printed from this material. As the ink is taken from more than one level of the block a thick soft packing must be used.

34

5 · Paper

In all forms of woodcut and lino-printing ink is transferred to paper by pressure; either by hand pressure or by the force of the press platen descending on the block. The clarity of the printed image will depend on the softness, absorbency and smoothness of the paper – any possessing all these qualities is excellent for your purpose.

Very broadly speaking three main types of paper are used:

1 RAG PAPER made from a base of shredded rag. Whatman and Barcham Green are among the best known makes of hand-made rag paper for print-making in Great Britain. A smooth surface is generally necessary; this is known as 'hot-pressed' – a process in manufacture where the slightly damped sheet is pressed between polished metal plates by heated rollers. The 'not' (not hot-pressed) and 'rough' finishes are generally impractical for print-making. The paper should be soft sized or unsized. Unsized rag paper is known as 'waterleaf'.

2 The JAPANESE PAPERS made from bamboo, the bark of the mulberry tree and other vegetable fibres, which have a soft silky surface. There are many kinds, Hōsho, Torinoko, Shoji and others, but Hōsho papers, made from the bark of the paper mulberry, are those most favoured by the Japanese. The Japanese names may not be in general use; in Great Britain they are normally distributed under T. N. Lawrence's reference numbers.

3 PAPER made from WOOD-PULP is generally of cheaper quality and forms the bulk of the paper used in commerce. It has normally a characterless surface when used for finished prints, but is widely used for proofing.

Of the great variety of papers that are on the market at the present time only comparatively few are in general use by the print-maker. No doubt sources exist that have not yet been tried. Of recent years, for example, some of the filter papers made for industry have proved of particular interest.

Good printing paper, such as waterleaf and thick Japanese, has a highly porous nature, similar in this respect to ordinary Kleenex or blotting paper. This results from the enclosure of air spaces by the long vegetable fibres giving remarkable powers of absorption. The oil or water from the ink is drawn by capillary action into these channels between the fibres, leaving a concentration of pigment on the surface of the paper. The presence of size hardens the paper, making it less absorbent, and therefore less receptive to the ink. A heavily sized paper should be avoided.

Some rag papers are too stiff for use when dry, but they are excellent for printing if they are damped. Damping is quickly and easily done in the following way. Lay two or three sheets of newspaper on a sheet of glass, plastic or piece of metal, such as an unwanted litho plate. Sponge over the newspaper with water and lay one or two sheets of your printing paper on top; place over this some more newspaper and sponge over as before and continue till the necessary number of sheets are moistened. Thus the dry printing paper is interleaved with wet newspaper; about three sheets of wet newspaper to two of dry printing paper. A further sheet of glass – or any non-absorbent material – is put on the pile which becomes evenly damped throughout within a short time. Weights placed on top will hasten this process.

To dry the paper the method is reversed. Dry newspaper is put between the sheets of damp printing paper. This process will have to be repeated before the printed sheets are quite dry. Any failure to dry your prints flat, under pressure, will result in cockled sheets. Paper left for several days in a state of extreme moisture may develop fungus spots.

When using undamped sheets – and most work today is printed on dry paper – the surface as already noticed should be as smooth as possible. Machine manufactured papers, however, such as Basingwerke and offset cartridge have a mechanical smoothness lacking in interest; by contrast the smoothness of good Japanese is soft, silky and alive.

For colour printing whiteness is always a desirable quality. Cream paper will kill the brilliance of blue or violet. Absolute whiteness gives clear radiance to any light transparent colour.

Machine-made printing papers are made in a variety of sizes. For the art teacher who may have to order paper in bulk the information with regard to size, quality and weight, supplied by such firms as Spicers, Bowaters and other large paper suppliers, is of the utmost value. He can do no better than send for any information such firms supply. In England a sheet of artists' hand-made paper is commonly

36

either 'Royal' (size 20″×25″) or 'Imperial' (size 22″×30″), but Japanese papers vary considerably in measurement. For large prints use outsize sheets of Japanese No. 150 (size 39″×27″), or cartoon cartridge or filter paper cut from the roll.

Paper is always less expensive bought in quantity; rather less costly bought by the quire (twenty sheets) and much less costly bought by the ream (five hundred sheets). The large distributors have now standardized the ream at this figure – until recently it would have been four hundred and eighty to a ream of hand-made paper or five hundred and sixteen to a ream of printing paper. Thickness of sheets is indicated by the weight per ream – 60 lb., 90 lb., and so on. This figure, however, is expressed in terms of weight per ream according to the size of sheet, therefore a small sheet of say 90 lb. will be thicker than a larger sheet of the same paper.

Rag paper is so expensive that print-makers sometimes order sheets with minor imperfections known as 'retree' or 'outsides'. Such paper is generally much less costly.

Sometimes machine-made papers can be bought at fractional cost from printers' auction sales. For information you must apply to an auctioneer specialising in printing works sales.

Most papers have a right and a wrong side; they are smoother on one side than the other. Normally the smooth side will give the best impression of your print. Hand-made rag paper may have a watermark, the maker's name or the words 'hand made'. The side of the sheet from which the words are read is considered by the maker to be the correct surface for printing.

Where possible hand-made paper is printed untrimmed to preserve the rough edge of the sheet. If trimming is necessary the sheet may be ripped to size along the blade of a steel rule.

Untrimmed Japanese paper may have a wandering irregular edge. One corner should be snipped with scissors to a clean right-angle, so that accurate registration is possible by the method described (Page 31 and Fig. 5).

Finally if you produce prints for sale by a dealer the paper should be strong enough to withstand normal conditions of stocking, such as handling in a pile of other prints, otherwise within a short time your print becomes creased and spoilt. For transit by post the paper should also be flexible enough to roll easily onto a tube. Certain types of paper become ridged under these conditions.

A good deal of tracing paper is used in the print studio. To save cost it should be bought in continuous rolls. Ordinary tracing paper is insufficiently transparent when laid over a dark surface. For increased transparency rub over with a mixture of oil and turpentine.

Plastic film, such as Kodatrace, being highly transparent would be an ideal tracing material if it were less expensive. But even a single sheet is useful; for pencil lines on Kodatrace can be cleaned off with ordinary scouring powder and warm water and the surface used again.

For Proofing
When using colour the proofing may be a long process, involving much waste of material. Trials are often made on the backs of spoilt prints and discarded proofs. In addition I recommend the following types of paper:

Newsprint
Thin Japanese
Imitation Japanese No. 3
Imitation Japanese No. 4
Engineers No. 9 Cartridge

For the Edition
Choice of paper obviously depends on many factors, type of blocks, printing method used, cost, length of edition, etc. The following papers are in fairly general use:

Whatman, Waterleaf
Barcham Green, Waterleaf
3 mm. Filter Paper
Hōsho, Thick Japanese
Hōsho, Medium Japanese
Shoji, Thin Japanese
Hodoruma, Japanese
Bugeawa, Textured Japanese
    white or various colours

For Students
Newsprint
Basingwerke
Lithographic offset cartridge
Sugar Paper
Brown Packing Paper
Imitation Japanese No. 3
Imitation Japanese No. 4

38

6 · Inks

Both water-colour and oil inks are used for linocut and woodcut. Traditionally the water inks have been most favoured but today the oil inks are also widely used. The water inks give a transparent flat effect; capable of great delicacy and unity but sometimes lacking in vitality.

Having more body the robuster oil inks, that may be used transparent or opaque, give a fuller range of quality and greater brilliance of colour. I would suggest that those starting work at print-making should try both: by extensive trial alone will these two different mediums give up their secrets.

If you run a print-making class it is an advantage to stock both types of ink. The water-colour inks dry quickly and are clean to work. But you may find your students prefer the oil inks, especially for innovation and experiment or for large vigorously carved blocks that demand a bold and vivid printed image.

Oil Inks

Oil printing ink is basically pigment or colouring matter ground up in boiled linseed oil with drying agents added. Of the hundreds of different materials used in modern ink manufacture the most important fall into three separate groups:

1 Pigments that give both colour and stiff consistency to the ink.

2 Varnishes or vehicles, chiefly linseed oil. This is the fluid portion which carries the grains of pigment, giving them binding power and assisting the drying of the ink.

3 Driers and reducing mediums. These are added either to speed drying, reduce stickiness or increase transparency.

Linseed oil, manufactured from the seed of flax, is normally about as stout as thin cream. For ink-making it is heated to high temperatures which result in the oil particles linking together into larger groups giving the oil the appropriate thickness. It dries by chemical action; absorbing oxygen from the air it will 'oxidize' to form a solid. Even in a thin film it takes several days to dry, but certain compounds of the metals lead, cobalt and manganese have the power to speed this process. Combined with rosin and other materials these metallic compounds, known as 'paste-driers', are those favoured by the print-maker; they will speed the drying process to a few hours.

The term 'drying' means merely turning from liquid into solid. In printing there are three ways in which this transformation is brought about:

1 By allowing the paper to soak up the ink.
2 By causing part of the ink to evaporate – as in the water content of the water inks.
3 By chemical change, such as the oxidization process already mentioned.

In practice the drying of inks has wide variations and many agents are used commercially to speed drying. It will be obvious, however, that in the early stages of proofing, when work must often move forward rapidly, the use of driers is fully justified; but any the print-maker uses for his finished work should be used sparingly – their effect may spoil the quality of the pigment on the paper.

A little boiled linseed oil is used to thin the printing ink, but if you add too much a yellow halo will slowly appear round the edges of the printed area as the oil discolours with time; this is known as bleeding. Vaseline, paraffin, petroleum jelly and ordinary oil paint are other agents used for thinning the colour, but commercial 'thinners' are not recommended.

Ink of good consistency will slip slowly from the palette knife; rolled evenly on the block it should glisten like silk, giving a light hissing sound beneath the stroke of the roller.

Any colourless matter added to the body of the ink will disperse the intensity of its colour. To make ink more transparent or lighter in tone a reducing or tinting medium is used – a sufficient quantity will dilute black or any colour to a thin transparent film. Reducing medium is of great use both for underprinting and for overall tone printing. A good quality letterpress reducing medium is in general use in my own studio.

Broadly speaking the colouring matter of all printing inks falls into four groups as follows.

Originally the materials for ink-making were taken from the earth, mostly from deposits containing iron. Umber ochre and sienna, the earth colours, were also the materials of the artist – even the prehistoric artist. For printing ink these earths were washed, dried, powdered and finally ground in oil. Sometimes they were burnt to produce changes of shade such as deeper, browner or redder tints; for black soot was used. To some extent these materials, known as natural pigments, are still used in ink-making.

Another group of pigments is sometimes called 'organic'; this we may take to mean connected with the organic processes of life. The colour sepia, a brownish black, is an example. It may be made from the ink of the cuttlefish, a fluid discharged by this sea creature when it is frightened. This discharge obscures the water with

40

an inky cloud enabling the cuttlefish to escape its enemies. Cochineal, a bright pink, is obtained from a tropical insect, madder and indigo from plants.

Another group of colours, dating from a much later stage in the history of ink-making, are those taken from mineral materials such as lead, to produce the chromes; colours that range from red through orange to bright clear yellow. From the metal chromium come the chromium oxide greens. Iron gives reds, browns and bronze blue, mercury and sulphur the scarlet pigment known as vermilion.

The most recent addition to the ink-maker's palette are the aniline dyes largely derived from coal tar. They are a chief feature of recent commercial ink manufacture. Certain blue and green pigments must be counted among the finest of these colours, monastral blue in particular, a cold transparent darkish blue, possessing unequalled light fastness and therefore permanence, while titanium white, an extremely opaque white pigment of fairly recent invention, is of special value in a colour used for printing on a dark ground.

Certain bright clear colours, such as red, pink and blue, even in inks of good manufacture, tend to fade on sustained exposure to bright light. If these colours are in regular use in your studio it is well worth while to ask your ink-maker to put up such pigments as cadmium red, cadmium yellow and monastral blue in the amount you need for these are colours that do not fade.

If you only need small quantities of ink you can get a range of colour from an engravers' supply store. Larger amounts should be bought by weight direct from an ink-maker of repute – Winstones and Mander Brothers are among firms of good standing. Colours vary so much in quality, and today their preparation is such a highly technical process, that to a great extent you are forced to trust the brand name.

You can sometimes get a quantity of ink at small cost at a printers' auction sale. These inks may be poor quality 'jobbing' inks, but they are a great economy in trial-and-error proofing. Ink can be safely stored over long periods; partly-used tins may form an air-proof crust preserving the colour beneath for future use.

The inks are sold in various forms, litho, half-tone, letter-press, gravure and many others. The letter-press inks are those most generally useful for woodcut and lino printing, but lithographic ink can also be used. The novice print-maker, starting out with only a few tubes of oil printing ink, can extend his range to some extent with ordinary oil colour.

Printing ink is sold in either tubes or tins. Tubes, though a little more expensive, are convenient storage for the studio; the ink will keep a long time if the caps are firmly screwed on. When a tin is opened, however, a large ink surface is exposed to the air and starts to harden. Some print-makers recommend protecting this with greaseproof paper, but in practice it is difficult to remove the ink evenly enough to make this effective.

It is sometimes felt that oil inks have an unpleasant gloss, but this can be avoided either by stripping or by the use of a highly absorbent surface such as the thick Japanese papers possess. To strip, place a sheet of newspaper or tissue paper over the block, re-register the print above it while the ink is still wet, and run your sheet through the press; but be careful to adjust the pressure to the amount of ink you want removed. Properly printed oil ink is semi-matt only when over-printed; it will then have a slight eggshell gleam. Thick soft papers will take up much more ink than less absorbent ones or those containing size. On certain types of heavy Japanese paper a block may even have to be re-inked and re-printed before you get an effective image.

When printing an edition it is extremely difficult to match colour to the original proof. To do this successfully you should leave some colour over from the original mix. This is at once carefully packaged in greaseproof paper, the edges are folded sharply in and bound with a rubber band. The colour can then be kept for many weeks. In a studio where various editions may have to be kept in print these colour packages are conveniently kept in marked cardboard boxes. When colour has to be re-mixed a little colour from the original sample is scraped out thin with a palette knife onto white paper. A sample of your new mix should then be scraped out beside this for direct comparison. This is nearly always necessary; for the solid mass of colour is likely to look quite different to the thin film of the same colour used for your print.

If no ink is left over from your original printing put sample colour swatches on a waste proof of your print, marking beside each the ingredients of the mix.

When it is necessary to match your colour direct from a proof, 'eye-holes' are used to isolate the tint to be matched from the surrounding areas of colour. An 'eye-hole' is simply a small hole cut in a sheet of white paper. This is placed on the print so that the colour to be matched shows through. A second 'eye-hole' is placed on a sample of your new mix and the two tints are compared.

Water-Colour Inks

Water-colour printing-inks, sometimes called aquatone inks, consist of dyes and pigments ground with a gum, glycerine-dextrine mixture. They dry partly by evaporation and partly by penetrating the paper. The colouring matters used are similar to those employed in oil ink manufacture. The high speed of drying of the water inks makes them particularly useful where an immediate over-printing is required.

42

7 · Rollers and Rolling-up

The ink roller, or brayer as it is sometimes called, is the standard instrument for inking the relief block, a process known as rolling-up. Its function is to apply an even film of ink to the printing surface; in passing it should be noticed that this film should normally be as thin as possible, provided it gives you the required intensity of tint. In use, the roller is gripped firmly but easily, and moved backwards and forwards over the block with a flexible wrist.

The effective inking of a block depends on many factors; the material used and its surface; the consistency of the colour; the type of paper; the pressure of the press. Experience, however, should quickly sharpen your instinct for the best method to follow for the inking of any particular block.

The stroke of the roller is three times its diameter – a two-inch roller gives you a six-inch stroke. To understand its action, load the roller evenly with black ink and press it firmly down on to a large sheet of paper. Now rotate it right across the surface. At the first complete turn you will see that most of the ink is already transferred to the paper; at the second rotation a much paler shade appears. At about the fourth, the ink on the paper is reduced to the lightest tone of grey. It will now be seen that reduction of the tint has taken place in a series of clearly defined steps, and not as a steady lightening of the original black. To ink any surface successfully the roller must pass across it many times; otherwise the 'steps' it leaves will show in the print. Only repeated rolling will give your block an even film of ink; large plain surfaces in particular need careful and repeated rolling.

The oil inks used in printing have the property of becoming more liquid – a little less sticky – if they are stirred with a palette knife or thoroughly rolled-up with the roller. As well as giving an even film, repeated rolling moves the ink rapidly over the face of the block producing the more liquid consistency that favours an effective printed image.

To sum up, roll the ink thoroughly on both inking slab and block; use the thinnest film of ink that will give the depth of colour needed. But when you are overprinting a darker colour the opacity as well as the depth of tint must be taken into account.

43

Only in special cases where you want a juicy surface or glossy colour of enamelled opulence – as in certain prints of Picasso – is the print achieved with a lavish supply of ink upon the block.

The best standard roller sold in London is either 4 inches or 6 inches wide. It is made of plastic on a metal core – a great improvement over the old gelatine model mounted on a core of wood. Both types of roller are expensive but the plastic one is more than worth the extra cost.

Gelatine rollers are not proof against heat; never leave them in the sun or near a radiator. They are not suitable for water-colour inks as they may take up moisture from the colour and soften. Their surface becomes rough with wear more easily than the plastic roller.

Rollers are supplied in frames of various patterns; the most practical are those that can be turned over when not in use and laid on the back of the frame.

The roller is not always well mounted in the brass bearing; but you may be able to adjust this with ordinary metal washers between roller and frame. A drop of oil may be used for smooth and silent running.

Their surface will also vary from moderately hard to a rubbery softness. The harder the roller the more it stays on the surface of the block, while the soft roller presses into the relief. If your block has delicate texture in slight relief, you need a roller with firm surface that will not squash into the shallow lines and pits.

Both plastic and gelatine rollers harden somewhat with use. If at first the surface of your roller is inconveniently soft and sticky, you may roll it up with black oil ink, very smooth and thin. Let it get perfectly dry and the tackiness will have gone; but the roller will retain a more perfect surface if you let it toughen slowly.

Be sure to choose the right size of roller for the area to be inked. If you are using several colours on one block, small rollers are used. These rollers, useful for both multi-colour printing and small fine-texture blocks, are generally made of hard rubber tubing on a wooden core and are quite inexpensive.

Rollers should be hung vertically when not in use. For this purpose you may find it convenient to screw small cup-hooks into the top of the wooden handles.

All rollers should be kept scrupulously clean; any ink left on them will harden and stick permanently. To clean, sprinkle cleaning fluid on the ink slab and roll till the ink is softened; wipe with a soft rag. Some print-makers powder with talc before storing the rollers away.

Sponges and padded leather dabbers, known as tampons, are occasionally used for inking the block. Linoleum and wood may also be inked with hog-hair brushes or housepainter's brushes. The texture of the brush marks, however, must be then considered as part of the print.

44

8 · Proofing and Printing

Printing from wood and lino is normally carried out in two separate stages, proofing and printing. First the block is proofed and when colour is used this is an activity no less creative than the cutting of the block itself. At this stage the latent possibilities of the block are discovered and developed and a proof produced that is a full and powerful expression of your blocks. Proofing, therefore, is accomplished with freedom and in a spirit of exploration and excitement.

Printing, on the other hand, is a much more formal procedure since your object is to obtain a series of perfectly matched prints from the working proof. It requires a high standard of order and disciplined craftsmanship. You will soon discover, however, that this discipline follows no single pattern. Different sets of colour blocks will need different treatment and sometimes this treatment is unique to that one print and is never repeated.

To proof wood or linoleum blocks, the ink is laid with a palette knife in a flat ridge at the top of the ink slab. You now approach the roller along the slab until a small quantity of ink is detached in a narrow strip. This is rolled into a thin and even surface, lifting the roller frequently to ensure good distribution, a process already described. The ink is now transferred to the block, using smooth and level movements.

Once the proof is pulled, it appears as a reverse image of the block: a 'mirror-reflection'. This is something peculiar to print-making. At first it may well be found disconcerting, but as adjustment is made, this reversal of the image may itself constitute a certain stimulus, since the slight unfamiliarity of the mirror image may allow the eye to assess its character with new force.

To explore the colour possibilities of your prints pieces can be cut from a set of proofs and fitted together differently. This may help you to develop alternatives and modifications free from the physically arduous work of entirely re-proofing your blocks.

With experience you are unlikely to attempt to get a finished proof of any one block before evolving your colour scheme as a whole. When you are successful, and your colour has vitality and depth, you are likely to discover that the proofing and correction of the block have gone along together. There is no clear point where the block is cut and the proofing begun; they are both part of a single process; but the print-maker must find out for himself the secrets of this give-and-take between block and image.

The colours of your proof are modified, sometimes entirely changed, when the order in which they are printed is altered. On the whole, I believe you will find the traditional procedure, light colours first and dark ones last, is the most generally useful. The final dark printing appears stronger if it goes down last, partly because the early printings have made the paper less porous and less absorbent; consequently the last printing appears slightly glossy. Light tints first, dark ones last; though this is a general rule followed by commercial printers it is there, like any rule, only to be disobeyed – disobeyed and forgotten by the artist-printer the moment it fails to serve his personal aim. Obviously enough for many colour schemes there is no call to stick closely to this order. Through experiment you will discover, in any case, that you can get some of the most interesting colour effects by printing solid, light, pure colour over dark colour – blue, orange or white, perhaps over black.

When printing an edition, the colour to be taken from any one block is printed down on all the sheets to be handled; these are then hung up to dry before the operation is continued. Normally oil ink should be touch-dry before overprinting; though a strong dark colour can generally be set down straightaway over a thin light colour.

Oil ink can, however, become too dry. If several weeks elapse between one printing and another there may be difficulty in getting the ink to take; this is known as 'refusing'. If this occurs try rubbing the surface to be reprinted with a solution of oxgall.

The printing inks have great variation in their transparency – the aniline dye colours are generally translucent – the earth colours and cadmiums generally opaque. Any colour, however, may be made less opaque with reducing medium, or more opaque with the addition of solid white. It is only by testing on the proof that you discover the value of any one colour in relation to the rest. Testing is done on the rolled-out ink by pressing a piece of white paper, with your thumb, and judging alongside the colour of the proof. Once on the block the colour will print lighter or darker, according to the pressure of the press. The tone printed is always the sum of pressure plus ink film.

For the Albion press, the blocks should be no thicker than nine-tenths of an inch, not more than type-high; English type is 0.917 of an inch high. The blocks can,

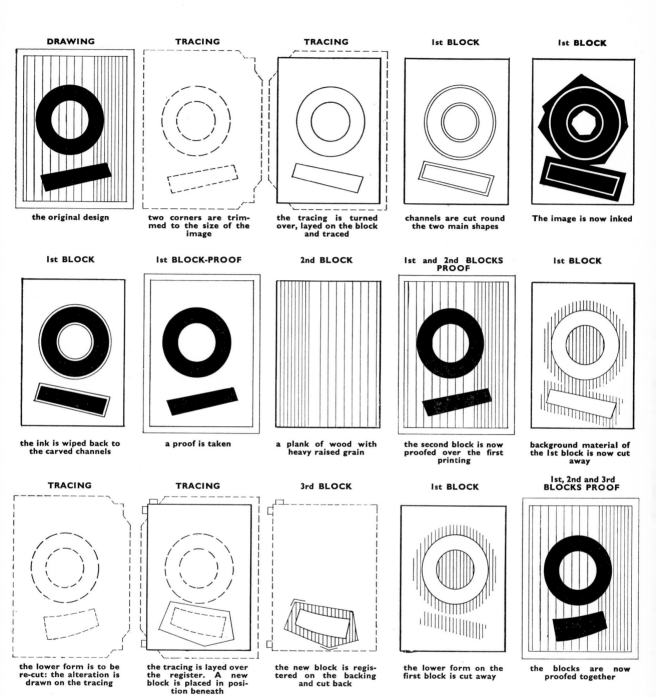

DRAWING	**TRACING**	**TRACING**	**1st BLOCK**	**1st BLOCK**
the original design	two corners are trimmed to the size of the image	the tracing is turned over, layed on the block and traced	channels are cut round the two main shapes	The image is now inked
1st BLOCK	**1st BLOCK-PROOF**	**2nd BLOCK**	**1st and 2nd BLOCKS PROOF**	**1st BLOCK**
the ink is wiped back to the carved channels	a proof is taken	a plank of wood with heavy raised grain	the second block is now proofed over the first printing	background material of the 1st block is now cut away
TRACING	**TRACING**	**3rd BLOCK**	**1st BLOCK**	**1st, 2nd and 3rd BLOCKS PROOF**
the lower form is to be re-cut: the alteration is drawn on the tracing	the tracing is layed over the register. A new block is placed in position beneath	the new block is registered on the backing and cut back	the lower form on the first block is cut away	the blocks are now proofed together

Figure 4 Some typical stages in the development of a woodcut shown in diagrammatic form. It will be obvious that in practice drawing and cutting are done boldly and informally

47

of course, be thinner. When you use thin blocks, however, such as plywood or linoleum, the bed of the press is packed up with boards of suitable thickness (Fig. 7, 1). A chipboard sheet, half an inch thick, and two pieces of hardboard, cut to fit the bed, are probably all you need.

The main adjustment of the height of your block can now be made by adding or removing one or more of these sheets of hardboard, or if a heavy plankwood block is to be printed, then the chipboard too will have to be removed (Fig. 7, 3). The packing under the block, the sheets of board that rest on the bed of the press,

Figure 5 Block shown on register. To raise the level of the paper register, when type-high blocks are used, pieces of card are glued to small pieces of wood

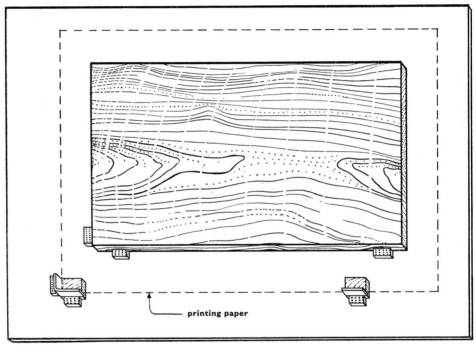

printing paper

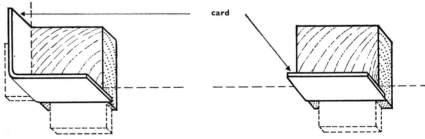

card

is for the main adjustment only. This will bring the height of your block to roughly the correct position in relation to the platen of the press, but it is only roughly – the fine adjustment must always be done with the paper packing on top of the block. This is the basic principle of all correct packing. Once thoroughly understood it will enable you to pack blocks of varying height both quickly and effectively, and give greater range in the choice of your materials.

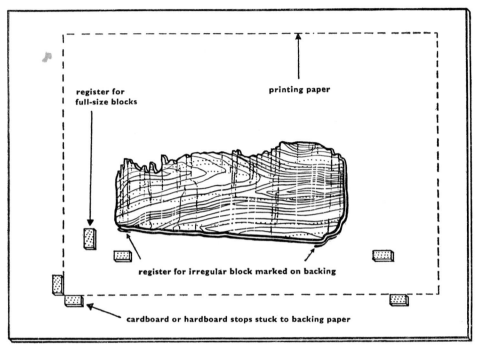

Figure 6 The placing of an irregular block is marked on the register. The method used to find the correct position in relation to your print is explained in Figure 4

Packing for the top of the block consists of thin material – manilla boards, sheets of cardboard or paper of varying thickness, stout or slim as the job demands. For this purpose a pile of waste proofs and suitable boards should be kept within easy reach of the press.

For work of a decorative nature, you can, of course, use top-packing of special texture; the canvas grain on the back of hardboard, for example or the texture of corroded metal. In this case your block will print with the pattern of such packing, but clearly the use of printing of this kind may well be quite unsuitable for more serious work.

The packing on top of the block must be adjusted for each separate printing. Thick soft packing such as felt, an etching blanket or a pad of newspaper will sink

49

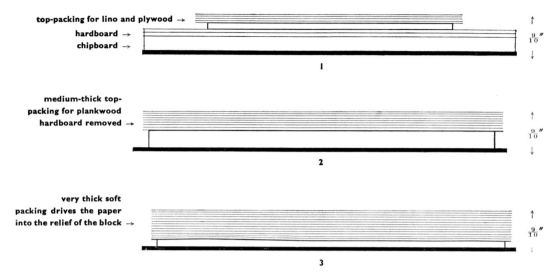

top-packing for lino and plywood →
hardboard →
chipboard →

1

medium-thick top-packing for plankwood
hardboard removed →

2

very thick soft packing drives the paper
into the relief of the block →

3

Figure 7 Packing

into the block, driving the paper firmly into its relief. This is used if either the surface of your block is uneven, a warped plank, for example, or if you wish the print to pick up ink from more than one surface, such as the marks left by shallow cutting on the background. In such cases extremely thick packing can be used; if necessary the boards below the block can be removed altogether and an equivalent thickness of soft packing placed beneath the tympan.

Thin packing, such as a sheet of paper or manilla card is used when you want a sharp image of texture and fine lines. In this case the sheet to be printed remains flat on the surface of the block.

When the platen is brought down on the block with great force the printed image will show as a raised pattern when the print is viewed from the back. Print dealers refer to this as 'braille'.

If you are printing from blocks of different thicknesses, always test the height for correct packing before inking. For large blocks, the tympan may be unscrewed from the bed, giving more room for manoeuvre beneath the platen.

When the image on your print shows unevenness of tone you should burnish the weak areas before removing from the block. Carefully done, this should bring the lighter patches to the needed strength.

If the platen is worn or imperfectly adjusted, giving more pressure in one part than another, you should turn the block right round on the bed of the press, without moving the register, and reprint. Normally, this gives more even distribution of pressure and consequently a more even film of ink. It is better still to check and adjust the platen, which should be exactly parallel to the bed. For this, take four pieces of wood one inch thick; each is placed at one corner of the platen, which is lowered and held firmly on the blocks. The nuts above, which should be previously loosened, are now screwed home.

When the block itself is underinked, place a weight on one side of the print, turning back the free half to re-ink with the roller. Repeat for the remaining half, removing the weight to the opposite side.

You will want to inspect your proof before removing from the block. This is also done by putting a weight on the back of the print, first one side and then the other, turning back the free flap to view the print. Never take a proof from the block before you have checked the inking, for once removed it may not be possible to re-register the sheet with absolute accuracy. With any suggestion of a double image the print is spoilt.

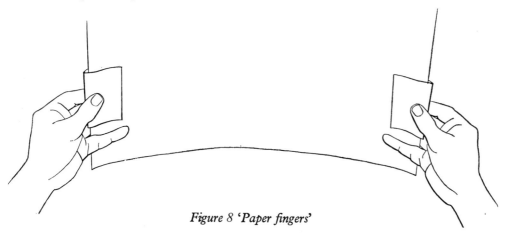

Figure 8 'Paper fingers'

Owing to the fact that your fingers are bound to get inky, all sheets are handled with cardboard clips, 'paper fingers', when you are printing either finished proofs or an edition. These are merely pieces of thin card of convenient size bent double. If a pile of these is kept on the press, their use quickly becomes automatic.

After printing the ink slab is carefully cleaned. Remove any thick ink with the palette knife, sprinkle a little paraffin on the slab and loosen the remaining ink with a pad of steel wool, finally wipe the surface clean with a few drops of petrol and rag.

Proofing without a Press: Burnishing

The artist or amateur without a press can still produce an effective image from his block by burnishing. To do this you merely apply pressure by rubbing on the back of the paper when the print is placed face downwards on the inked block.

American and Japanese print-makers, specialists in the woodcut, regard hand-rubbing as the finest way to print, largely because it enables you to vary the pressure from part to part, adding greater tonal expression to the finished proof.

You can burnish with any smooth rounded object that is easily grasped. A large hardwood salad spoon is excellent, but for small work some print-makers prefer a plated or silver spoon, either the belly of the spoon itself or the flat portion of the handle. You can also buy a specially made burnisher from a dealer; but the Japanese instrument known as a baren, about five inches in diameter, slightly convex on the under side, and covered with a lightly oiled bamboo sheath to travel smoothly over the paper, is normally unobtainable in this country.

When burnishing, a sheet of thin paper or card is placed between the spoon and the proof to protect the back of the print. In the classic Japanese method a square of slightly waxed card was used; but if you are using a thin absorbent Japanese paper you may want to see the image emerge through the paper as you work. The stroke of your burnisher should be smooth and even; the pressure is varied as the inking of the proof requires.

When you burnish with firm strokes a soft paper is driven partly into the relief of the block. The impact of the flat platen of the press, however, unless a pad of soft packing is used, takes an impression from the top surface only. Press printing and hand printing are to a great extent different processes, but certain advantages are attached to each. A press print finished by hand may well be found to provide the fullest control, certainly where close tonal modulation is needed for your print.

Other Methods

For linoblocks there is another method of printing without a press. Place the sheet of paper to be printed face upwards on the floor with a pad of newspaper beneath; the block is then placed face downwards on the sheet – the register is done from the corners by sight. Pressure is now applied by standing on top of the block; standing and stamping carefully with one foot, keeping the other stationary to grip the block in position. This procedure, surprisingly enough, is more effective than it sounds, certainly for a thickly inked block. Though accurate register is difficult, it gives a broad and strong effect, lacking in subtlety but not unkind to blocks that are broadly and strongly cut. Edward Bawden showed me this method, one with which he produced some outstanding prints before acquiring a press.

Lastly, you may get a broad image of your print, at an early stage of proofing when the block is partly cut, by inking the wood or lino heavily and merely applying pressure to the back of the paper with firm strokes of the printing roller.

PLATE 6 Paul Gauguin *Auti te Pape*. Woodcut
(Collection Museum of Modern Art)

PLATE 7 Paul Gauguin *Noa Noa*. Woodcut
(Collection Museum of Modern Art)

54

PLATE 8 Wassily Kandinsky *Kleine Welten 5.* Colour Woodcut

PLATE 13 Ernst Ludwig Kirchner *Portrait of Otto Mueller*. Woodcut

PLATE 14 Michael Rothenstein *Blue Circle*. Woodcut and Linocut

PLATE 15 Michael Rothenstein *Black and Red 1*. Woodcut and Linocut

PLATE 16 Michael Rothenstein *Liquitio*. Etched and engraved in Linoleum.

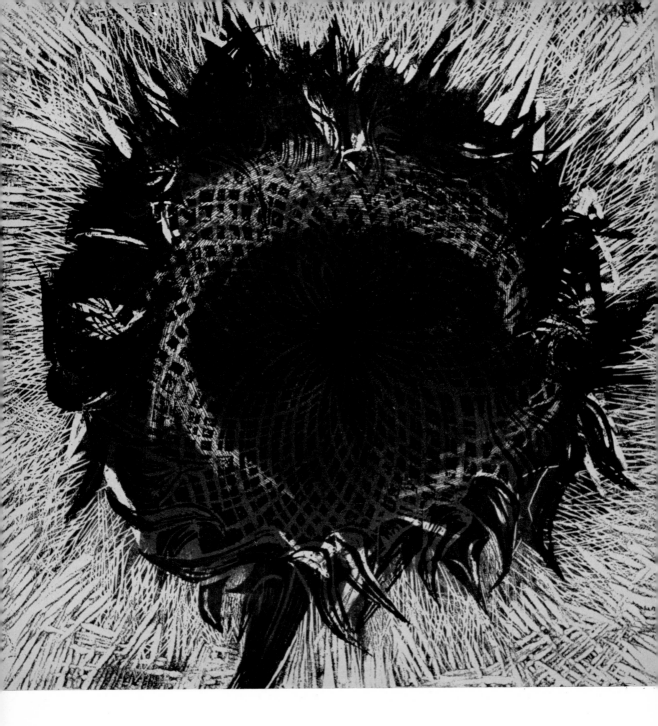

PLATE 19 Edward Middleditch *Sunflower*. Hardboard cut

66

PLATE 20 Henri Matisse *Seated Nude.* Linocut

(*Collection Museum of Modern Art*)

PLATE 21   Maurice Vlaminck *L'Aqueduc*. Woodcut

PLATE 22 Ernst Ludwig Kirchner
Self-portrait with Wife. Woodcut

PLATE 23 Erich Heckel
Standing Woman. Woodcut

69

PLATE 24 Lyonel Feininger *Fishing Fleet*. Woodcut

PLATE 25 Emil Nolde *Fishing Boat*. Woodcut

PLATE 26 Emil Nolde *Tanzsaal im 1906/07*. Woodcut

PLATE 27 Lyonel Feininger *Fishermen*. Woodcut

PLATE 28 Shiko Munakata from the '*Kegon Sutra*' suite. Woodcut

PLATE 29 Shiko Munakata from the '*Demons' Gate*' suite. Woodcut

PLATE 30 Erich Heckel *Im Atelier*. Woodcut

PLATE 31 K. Schmidt-Rottluff *Prophet*.
Woodcut

PLATE 32 Emil Nolde *Kerzentänzerinnen*.
Woodcut

PLATE 33 Pablo Picasso *Baccanale au Hibou.* Linocut

PLATE 34 Pablo Picasso *Picador, Femme et Cheval*. Linocut

PLATE 35 Shiko Munakata *Flower Hunting Mural*. Woodcut

76

PLATE 36 Gertrude Hermes *The Goat*. Linocut

PLATE 37 Pablo Picasso *Tête de Femme*. Colour Linocut

PLATE 38 Pablo Picasso *Femme couchée et Guitariste*. Colour Linocut

PLATE 39 Pablo Picasso *Baccanale au Taureau*

PLATE 40 Terry Spinks (aged 12) *Elephant*

PLATE 41 Pablo Picasso *Femme regardant par la Fenêtre.* Colour Linocut

PLATE 42 Pablo Picasso *Avant la Pique*. Colour Linocut

PLATE 43 Pablo Picasso *Mère, Danseur et Musicien.* Colour Linocut

9 · The Edition

Editions in colour taken from wood and linoleum blocks may vary from a few proofs only to a large series of exactly matched and numbered sheets. Very broadly speaking these editions are of three kinds.

1 The small edition of, say, twenty-five prints or under, printed entirely by the artist. When taken from the woodblock the sheets may be printed by hand-burnishing, or press-printed and finished by hand.

2 The average press-printed edition, twenty-five to seventy-five prints, printed in the artist's workshop, often with outside help.

3 Editions such as the linocuts of Picasso printed in France by the Spanish printer Arnera. Such editions are produced entirely by the professional printer in his own studio workshop.

The conditions existing in Paris and in certain workshops in the South of France – where the artist is able to call on help from highly skilled and experienced professional printers – are quite unique. In no other country, certainly no other European country or the Americas, can the print-maker hope to get assistance of any such quality. As a producer of editions – apart from the relatively inexpert help of student or trainee print-maker – he is on his own. The quality of the finished prints, as well as the creation of the design, is in the artist's hands alone; and since in this case both image and final printed sheets are close expressions of the artist's personality, it follows that the small artist-printed edition, taken from the relief block, must be considered as one of the most interesting, authentic and typical expressions of the print at the present time.

Under present conditions in Europe, America and most countries trading under conditions of capitalism, the signing and numbering of an edition remains a useful protective device for artist, dealer and purchaser alike. The print is generally numbered at the bottom left-hand corner of the image, 1/50, 2/50 and upwards: the second figure representing the total of the edition excepting the artist's proofs. These proofs should not exceed from five to ten per cent of the edition. They should be signed as such; strictly speaking they should be numbered either in Roman numerals or by the letters 'A' – 'B' – 'C' and so on, to differentiate such proofs from the main run of the edition.

In Great Britain editions of over seventy-five copies are liable to purchase tax.

The artist should resist the temptation of overrunning an edition when a further demand exists for his print. For goodwill to be established between artist, dealer and buyer it is necessary to respect the declared ceiling of the edition.

The Editions Alecto gallery, London, plays a special part in promoting British prints. Following the record of St. George's Gallery, earlier, this firm produces a continuous series of editions; perhaps the most notable have been the work of Eduardo Paolozzi and David Hockney. The Marlborough Gallery and Curwen Press have also published some fine editions. In the United States a growing public has been encouraged to buy original prints through such organizations as the International Graphic Arts Society of New York, the Philadelphia Print Club and the Museum of Modern Art.

A method should be found by the artist of keeping track of all numbered prints in the edition. In my own studio the sheets are generally printed off in batches of ten to twenty copies; the numbers are then recorded on a board, the studio battle-map, kept hanging on the workshop wall.

In addition to such records the artist should attempt to keep one copy – if possible, one perfect proof copy – of each print for his personal collection. Not only are these examples of potential value in relation to future retrospective exhibitions and loans but the very fact of their presence in the studio will help to maintain – and to surpass – the artist's own standards of accomplishment. Conversely it is very dispiriting to be left with only the poorest examples of your own prints.

The dealer takes $33\frac{1}{3}\%$ commission on the sale of prints; but when they are sold by the first dealer, through another gallery to a second dealer the commission can be as high as 50% since both galleries concerned may well want a 25% share. If, on the other hand, the dealer buys the edition outright, the artist generally accepts something less than half its total value; while the dealer on his side accepts all risk for the unsold copies of your print. Public purchase can also mean a lower profit to the artist; museums, museum services, County Councils and Education Committees may expect a 10% discount.

86

10 · Print Methods for Schools

Figure 9 Linocut by child of 10

Though my own experience of teaching younger students and children has been limited, a good deal of technical print-making research has been carried out – and still goes on – in the graphic studio at Great Bardfield. These activities have suggested a number of simple and direct techniques that can be easily mastered by younger age groups. They are given here with some chosen methods used by my colleagues at Camberwell Art School, but no doubt a number of the exercises and techniques suggested are now widely known and recognized by art instructors in many countries.

Effective printing blocks, as we have seen, can be made from a large variety of materials; in practice, however, the methods adopted will depend to a great extent on the resources of the school stockroom. In addition to linoleum, blocks can be made from hardboard, cardboard and some of the other materials described in earlier sections.

Printing surfaces for young students can also be made from a host of oddments, materials such as deckchair canvas, sacking, muslin, paper, string, tinsel, leaves and offcuts of leather. It may well be that the students themselves, pricked with enthusiasm, may help the teacher in the search for novel materials; scouring the attic, the back-yard or the wastepaper basket.

The school, however, will find it necessary to stock the glues and other adhesives that enable these flimsy materials to be used, as all of them need sticking to the face of the block. The animal glues, glue size and carpenters' glue, conveniently used as pearl glue, are excellent, but these need heating before use. Cold setting glues of several kinds are now, however, easily available. For small blocks Seccotine is a practical adhesive: for sticking metal foil to the block Araldite is of unequalled strength. But among the most remarkable recent additions to the stock of possible block-making materials are the emulsion paint bases. Some of these will combine into a solid surface with textiles, paper, canvas, woodshavings – and many other absorbent materials – hardening them. These can be inked and printed with oil pigments in the normal way. I would specially recommend the emulsion known in England as '617';* but similar substances are now obtainable in most countries.

The method whereby textiles, paper and other materials are stuck to a block – known as relief collage – offers an unequalled chance of experiment with novel surfaces, a challenge to which most young students show excited response.

In cutting lino and hardboard the danger of sharp tools is sometimes exaggerated. A child quickly learns to handle tools with dexterity and good sense. Sharp tools that cut easily are safer than dull ones that need forcing.

* Obtainable in gallon cans from Printa Inks, Neogene Works, Carlton Bridge, Great Western Road, London, W9. Unibond is a form more generally obtainable.

88

In several groups at Camberwell School the print is used in combination with poster-colour painting, collage and various other techniques. Plate 49 shows letter forms printed from separate blocks freely combined in a single print. It has been suggested that group efforts might be tried on an altogether larger scale. Each student for example might be asked to design and cut a lino block of a bird, fish, insect or mammal. The blocks could then be printed independently and each of the images snipped out with scissors. Finally, they could be assembled and stuck down upon an enormous painted landscape, birds in trees and clouds; insects and butterflies on bushes; fishes in ponds and lakes; animals in fields and forests.

Figure 10 Julian Rothenstein, aged 9 Linocut

Peggy Angus has used the lino block for group activities in a rather different way. As an example: each student was asked to carve a design on a standard piece of lino, six inches square, to be used as a repeat. The patterns used were always extremely simple: circles, lines, squares and dots in various combinations. The colour schemes were of equal simplicity – red on black, dark blue on light blue, red on yellow, black on white, etc. The most successful were later chosen and printed down, as repeats, on sheets of newsprint. These sheets were then pasted edge to edge, like wallpaper, to form large decorative panels for the school corridors. The effect was remarkable, reminding one of the diaper repeats once used on cathedral walls.

If more than one colour is used for his print, the young student should employ the method of block registration recommended on page 31. But for children, the simplest plan is to cut the sheet to the size of the block. To register his work the child should place the left-hand corner of the sheet carefully on the left-hand corner of the block, aligning the paper along the bottom edge before lowering on to the inked surface. Always register from the same corner in case either the block or sheet of paper are not accurately trimmed. A second method is to cut pieces out of the sheet as shown below.

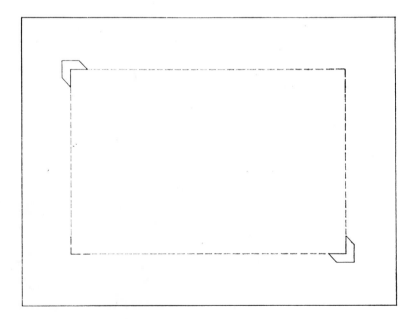

Figure 11 Register for a child

Figure 12 Child of 12 Torn paper print

Torn Paper (Figs. 12 and 13)

This is the simplest of all the methods described. Shapes are cut or torn from paper and laid on a piece of hardboard or lino. A heavily inked roller, pressed down firmly, is now passed over the block – once only – from edge to edge. The paper fragments, which will stick to the roller as it turns, act as masks, leaving parts of the lino bare. These read as white shapes when printed.

Anything that will lie flat on the block can be employed: leaves, pressed flowers, a piece of cotton or thread (Figs. 13 and 14).

The blocks may be printed by handrubbing with a spoon or in the Albion press. Oil ink gives the sharpest image.

Figure 13 Child of 12
Cotton and torn paper print

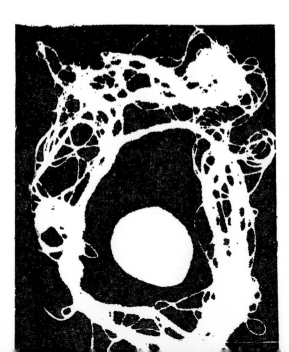

Figure 14 String print

Inking-up and Pressing Down

Ink up any suitable shape with a relief texture, using oil ink on the roller. Place the inked surface face down on the paper. Using a clean roller press the back firmly, while holding it in position with the free hand. Lift the edge to see if the image has printed clearly. Almost any flat pliable material can be used:

Embossed wallpaper	Leaves
Canvas, net or other fabric with a coarse weave	Pressed flowers
Textured cover papers	Cork mats
Oddments of woven cane from a broken chair	Off-cuts of leather
Sections cut from a rubber sponge	A ball of rag, etc.

Offset

Using a roller, ink a relief texture such as a coin or leaf; now take a second roller – this must be perfectly clean – and pass it steadily, once only, over the inked surface. It should pick up a perfect image. Offset by rotating the roller again, pressing firmly on your sheet of paper. Use a smooth plastic roller; to get a sharp detailed result great care is needed.

92

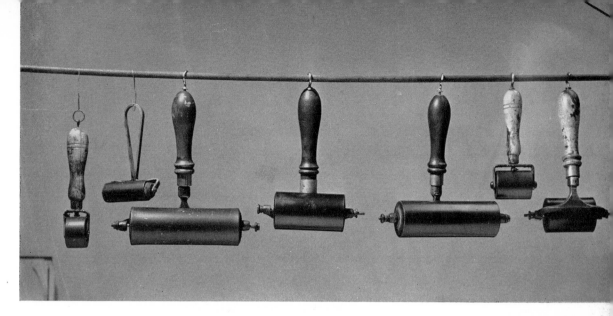

PLATE 44 Printing rollers

PLATE 45 Woodblock on register; the lower stops are to register the paper

93

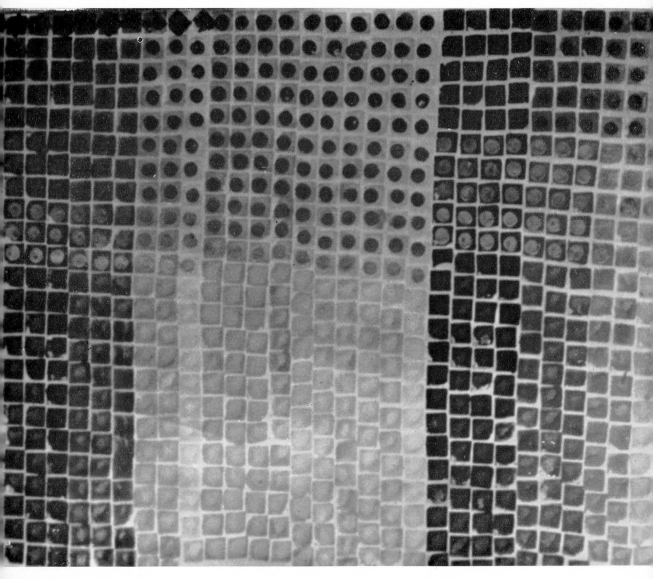

PLATE 46 | Jesu Watts, LCC Camberwell School of Art *Multiple Monoprint*

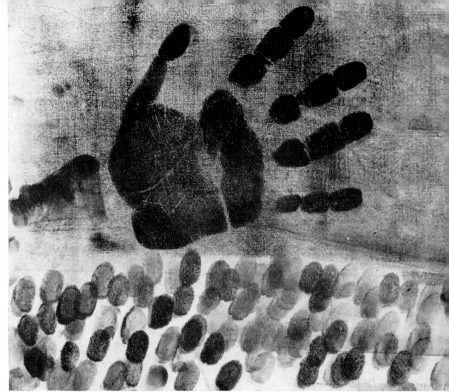

PLATE 47 Child aged 12
Direct print: hand and finger
prints

PLATE 48 Child aged 12 *Relief Collage*

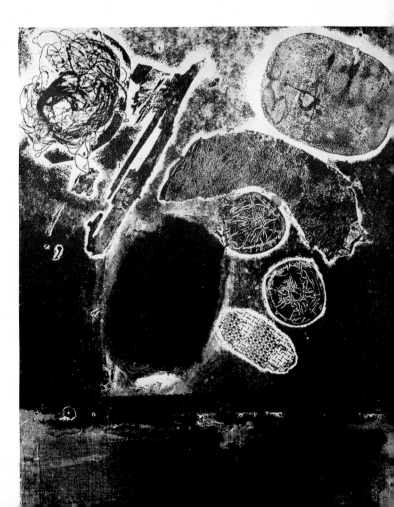

PLATE 49 Intermediate student, LCC Camberwell School of Art. Linocut

Figure 15 Chloë Cheese, aged 8 Cardboard print

Relief Collage (Plate 48)

Textured shapes, cut as necessary, are arranged and stuck to a block of lino or ply-wood with a strong glue such as Seccotine. Use anything that will stick close and flat. Weights should be placed on the collage until the glue is dry. The block is inked and printed in the normal way. When using a platen press a pad of soft packing should be placed above the block. Suggested materials:

> Sacking, Cardboard, Matches, Embossed paper, Foil and silver paper, Flattened milk bottle tops, Wood shavings, Dried leaves.

Paper-Cut Prints (Plate 40)

Silhouettes are cut from paper and pressed down on to stiff printing ink, or fabric ink, rolled evenly on the slab. The paper is now inked with the roller while thus stuck down; to avoid tearing the edge of the silhouette, the inking is done from the centre outwards. The inked paper can now be raised from the slab by inserting a knife-blade underneath. It is lifted and placed on a sheet of newspaper and the

97

printing paper is placed on top. The printing is done by rubbing the back of the sheet with the handle or belly of a spoon. This method offers great freedom; cutting with knife and scissors produces sharp, active shapes and the resulting image may possess unusual vivacity.

Unless a system of registration is used, by marking out the backing paper, the print cannot be accurately repeated and should be considered as a monoprint technique.

Another method of using the paper-cut: the main shapes of the design are drawn on fairly stiff paper; these are now cut out and inked in any desired colour with a roller. The separate pieces are laid on a fresh sheet – inkside downwards – and are printed either by burnishing or pressing with the roller. As the various pieces of the picture were cut from a single sheet, they will again fit together, producing the original image in reverse – a vigorous jig-saw of separately printed colours.

The Multiple Monoprint (Plate 46)

This extremely simple method is merely a development of the traditional stick printing technique.

A small piece of lino is cut to form a square, diamond, circle or similar basic shape. The block is printed by holding it in the fingers of one hand and inked with poster colour by a brush held in the other. The block is then pressed down on the sheet; the inking and pressing down continues until the image or pattern is complete.

The entire design thus built up of small repeated units – producing effects that are often curiously reminiscent of the pointillist – may possess the glitter of a mosaic, vibrant and rich.

The Cardboard Print (Fig. 15)

In its simplest form the block for this type of print is made by cutting shapes out of thick cardboard and pasting them down on a cardboard or hardboard base. From these shapes, the 'ups' of the block, the print is taken.

In a more sophisticated form papers of various texture are used. These are easily obtainable in great variety; the embossed papers used for note-book and catalogue covers; embossed wall papers sometimes known as 'lincrusta', obtainable from old wallpaper sample books; the corrugated papers of many sorts used for wrapping and packing; metal foils such as silver and tinsel paper. In addition, thin papers can be crumpled in the hand, then flattened out and pasted down, to form relief surfaces of extraordinary variety.

98

Figure 16 Intermediate students, L.C.C. Camberwell School of Art, Linocut repeating designs

These materials are assembled, cut out, and stuck down on the block as the student wishes. The surface of the block should be rubbed over or dabbed with a mixture of linseed oil and turpentine used rather sparingly and allowed to dry, or hardened with emulsion '617'. Oil inks alone should be used for printing. After use, the ink may be allowed to dry on the block to harden its surface.

Gesso Relief

A simplified form of the gesso relief method already suggested can be used successfully for young students. Plaster and pearl glue prepared as already described (page 34) are heated together to the consistency of paste or thick cream. While still warm, the mixture is spread on the block with knife or large brush; as the mixture cools and stiffens it can be drawn into with a stick, scraped and modelled with a knife and textured in any way you like. Leave overnight to dry. Once set, it can be sandpapered smooth or carved with gouges. Print normally by rubbing with a spoon or using the press. For the latter soft packing above the block is needed – the higher the relief the more padding will be needed.

The Elimination Method (Plate 13)

Among other artists Picasso has made superb use of this method. His example, indeed, might well make one hesitate to place an account of this technique in the section devoted only to the work of children and young students. Nevertheless, I believe it is here, in the class where so much jubilant experiment is tried, that this approach is likely to find its greatest value.

In this technique a single block of lino is used for all the colours. The plain square of lino is first printed down as a solid colour surface; this should be printed on several sheets of paper if you plan to repeat the image or to experiment with the colour. At the second stage, using the same piece of lino, cut any lines or shapes you want with knife or gouge. The block is now inked again and printed, in register, over the first colour. Stage by stage the block is now cut back and the various colours printed successively over the existing work.

It will be obvious that a sufficiently large number of prints should be taken at the early stages so that each of the prints in turn may be overprinted. Finally, a block is left with only sufficient lino to print the last colour.

If light colours are to be printed on top of dark ones, oil inks should be used.

The simplicity of this method makes it of special value to children. Prints, in colour, may easily suffer from over-deliberate planning; something that kills spontaneity and leads to rigidity of design; but this technique, with its commitment to direct cutting, encourages a bold and flexible approach.

100

List of Tools, Equipment and Materials

THOSE MARKED WITH AN ASTERISK (*) ARE THE BASIC TOOL KIT

Tools and Equipment	Purpose
*Stanley knife with heavy-duty blade ⎱ Japanese woodcutting knife ⎰	For scoring; cutting V lines; trimming lino; and setting down
*V tool or scrive	Cutting lines
*Round gouges, various sizes from $\frac{1}{8}''$ to $\frac{3}{4}''$	Cutting broad lines; general carving and clearing of the block
Woodcarving gouges, size 1″ and over, mounted in short handles. Round and extra flat	Carving large plankwood blocks
Multiple tool	Cutting close parallel lines
Wood saw	Cutting plankwood and plywood
Large chisel	Trimming edge of plankwood
Stanley wood plane	Truing face of plankwood
Albion or press of similar platen type	Proofing; printing; stripping excess ink from the impression; offsetting
Etching press	As above if platen press not available, and for 'aquatinting' lino
*India carborundum oil stone; axolite stone	Sharpening knives, gouges and other cutting tools
Washita stone; Arkansas stone	Sharpening woodcutting tools to extra keen edge
*Slip-stones; various sizes	Sharpening the inside of hollow gouges
Small grindstone	Grinding worn edge of bevel of gouges and chisel
Leather strop, dressed with razor strop (carborundum) paste	Maintaining edge of woodcutting tools
*Oil-can	Dressing the oil stone
Electric drill with sander attachment	Graduating surface of wood; clearing shallow-cut backgrounds for plywood
Wire brush attachment for electric drill	Heightening wood grain; cleaning away decayed or bruised wood-fibres when old wood is used
Wire brush	Cleaning old wood; heightening grain
Circular saw attachment for electric drill	For cutting plankwood and plywood rapidly and easily
Large steel square	Measuring and cutting blocks true
Steel straight edge	Setting out blocks; trimming lino; trimming and ripping paper
Metal G cramps	Gripping wood blocks in position while working

Large metal weights	Gripping block while working; gripping prints or tracings on block
Small metal weights	Most other purposes for which drawing pins are normally used
*6″, 4″ and 3″ plastic rollers in brass frames	Inking the block
Small rubber and composition rollers	Inking small or close-together surfaces when more than one colour is used on the block
Hog hair brushes	Inking small surfaces; working on proof or block with oil printing ink
Indian ink	Staining wood or lino block for tracing with yellow carbon paper
Yellow carbon paper	Tracing on dark surfaces
Black carbon paper	Tracing on light surfaces
*Ink slab	Rolling out printing ink
*Palette knives – various sizes	Spreading and mixing printing ink
Carpenter's pencil	Drawing on wood
Chalk or pastel	Drawing on dark surfaces
Glue pots	Warming glue and glue gesso
Pearl glue, glue size or carpenter's glue	Making gesso
Glasspaper, various grades	Smoothing plankwood and plywood
Steel wool	Cleaning blocks
Ball-clip drying rack	Hanging prints upright to dry
Clothes brush or paperhanger's brush	Dusting blocks
Sprinkler containers	Cleaning fluids
*Large hardwood salad spoon or metal or agate burnisher	Burnishing
Tinman's snips	For shaping edges of free-form lino blocks

Some Sources of Graphic Supplies

Inks

California Ink Co.
2939 East Pico Boulevard
Los Angeles
California

Cronite Co. Inc.
35 Park Place
New York, N.Y.

Interchemical Corp.
Printing Ink Division
175 Albany Street
Cambridge, Mass.

T. N. Lawrence and Son
2 Bleeding Heart Yard
Greville Street
London, E.C.1

Mander Bros.
2 Noel Street
London, W.1

Winstone Ltd
150 Clerkenwell Road
London, E.C.1

Paper

Barcham Green
  (hand-made papers)
Hayle Mill
Maidstone
Kent

Chicago Cardboard Co.
1240 N. Homan Avenue
Chicago 51

Geliot Whitman Ltd
  (tracing paper)
16A Herschell Road
London, S.E.23

Japan Paper Co.
100 East 31st Street
New York 16, N.Y.

T. N. Lawrence and Son
  (hand-made papers, filter papers,
  newsprint)
2 Bleeding Heart Yard
Greville Street
London, E.C.1

Nelson Whitehead Paper Corp.
7 Laight Street
New York 13, N.Y.

Spicers Ltd
  (machine-made papers)
19 New Bridge Street
London, E.C.4

Technical Paper Corp.
28 Huntingdon Avenue
Boston 16, Mass.

Presses

Edwin Evans
  (printing works auctioneers)
149 Fleet Street
London, E.C.4

Kimbers Supplies Service
44 Clerkenwell Green
London, E.C.4

W. C. Kimber
25 Field Street
London, W.C.1

T. N. Lawrence and Son
2 Bleeding Heart Yard
Greville Street
London, E.C.1

Tools

Apex Printers' Roller Co.
  (rollers)
1541 North Sixteenth Street
St. Louis 6, Mo.

Buck and Ryan
  (carving tools, woodworking tools)
310 Euston Road
London, N.W.1

Craftools Inc.
396 Broadway
New York, N.Y.

T. N. Lawrence and Son
  (gouges and rollers)
2 Bleeding Heart Yard
Greville Street
London, E.C.1

E. C. Muller
61 Frankfort Street
New York, N.Y.

Wild and Stevens Inc.
  (rollers)
Boston Post Road
Orange, Conn.

Index to technical references in text